Under a Rock

AN ELECTROSENSITIVE SURVIVAL GUIDE

By Julia Lupine

Copyright © 2023 Julia Lupine
Cover by Paul-Hawkins.com
All Rights Reserved

Table of Contents

Welcome to Electromagnetic Hell 8
What is Electrosensitivity? 10
What is Electrosensitivity not? 12
Who becomes Electrosensitive? 16
Dangers of Wireless Radiation 18
My Early Life as an Electrosensitive Refugee 20
Why Me? 26
Types of Dark Force Machines and How to Deal with Them 30
The Meters 43
The Satan Tree 47
Dark Force Energy 49
The Tin Foil Hat 53
Gary 57
Electricity and Life 62
A Typical Day for a Desert Rat 66
This is your Brain on Twitter 70
EMF School, Day One 74
The Alpha Levels 80
But I thought only Ionizing Radiation has Negative Biological Effects? 85
Day to Day Variation in Sensitivity 86
Double-Blind-Studies---versus. Observational Awareness 88
Double-Blind Proof 90
Electricity in the Medical Mainstream 92
Bliss Ninnies 94
Inconsistency of Belief 103

How *not* to talk to people who don't understand 105
Psychology of Electrosensitives........................ 110
Diet and Electrosensitivity 113
Wireless Refugee... 123
Gut Problems: Universal with EHS 128
Phase Shift... 132
Vermont... 134
Chemical Sensitivity 139
The Yankee Candle Factory 142
Doing my Best... 144
Herbalism for EHS 148
Grounding.. 163
Grounding Technologies 165
The Day Everything Changed 170
The Invisible Fence 174
The Abandoned House 179
Chaga Dreams 186
The Long Winter 190
The Amtrak 196
Desert Rat Hits Rock Bottom............................ 200
A Serendipitous Meeting................................... 204
The Hospital 206
The Farm 208
Homesteading.. 212
An Unexpected Turn of Events......................... 218
2021 221
Electrosafe Building Solutions.......................... 223
Living with Electricity (as Safely as Possible) How to Hardwire Internet 233

Third World Magic Fridge 237
Clothing and Bedding... 239
Pack Goats... 243
5G Rollout.. 245
Know Your Enemy: What's up with Elon Musk?
.... 249
Birds and Electromagnetism 254
Electrosensitivity in the Media......................... 259
The Body Electric,... 261
or Reprogrammable Hardware? 261
Desert Rat makes a Nest................................... 267
Are you Electrosensitive?.................................. 272
References 274
Bibliography.. 276

Prologue

Somewhere deep in the wilds of the Utah desert, I raise the rock and bash my cell phone to smithereens. Die, Dark Force Machine, I think, you and all you stand for.

The digital leash that formerly connected me to the world out there: honking horns, florescent lighting, and that horrible aisle at the grocery store that reeks of vile substances labeled things like "Tide" and "Glade." Resumes. Traffic cameras. Receipts the cashier hands you that are permeated with Bisphenol-A, a toxic chemical that causes hormonal disturbances and if you tell the cashier that, she looks at you with glassed-over eyes like a cow munching Monsanto corn in a feedlot.

Smash, and the screen caves in. No more chirping bird text messages. Smash. No more headaches from the electromagnetic frequencies these things put out. Smash. The front panel busts open and I can see computer chips. This thing is taking forever to die.

I give it one more good whack. Battery acid sizzles into the sand like brains. I scoop sand over the dead pieces like a cat burying a turd. Maybe archaeologists of the future will dig it up and puzzle over why these devices made our civilization fall.

More likely I'll dig it up myself and discard the pieces once it stops smoking (Probably should have taken out the battery first, I think. I'll remember that for next time).

Satisfied, I wipe my hands on my camo pants and walk barefoot into the desert. I think about the repercussions and the people I'm going to piss off by my actions. My editor. My parents back East. My friends, who already think I'm crazy and paranoid because I say I feel physically sick when I talk on a cell phone. It's all in your head, they say. Why do you have to be such an extremist?

Everything to extremes, I say. It's the bipolar way. The desert is gray this morning and the road is dusty.

I don't know where I'm going from here.

Welcome to Electromagnetic Hell

Electromagnetic Frequency Hypersensitivity, or EHS as I will call it for the sake of brevity, is one of the weirdest and least understood phenomena of the modern age. We've all heard the rumors that cell phones are bad for us, and of studies that show that people who live near high-voltage power lines are more likely to develop cancer. And indeed, most people are willing to believe this to some extent. We are, we all know, surrounded by carcinogens (especially in the state of California).

"Just one day closer to death," folks say with a smile. "It's all gonna kill us sooner or later."

Most people also are willing to believe that continual eating of Little Debbie Cakes may eventually lead to diabetes. "But everything in moderation," they say, and for most people, that works. Eat kale in your smoothie the next morning, go for a jog before work.

For a diabetic, however, just one Ho Ho can spell disaster. Likewise, for a real electrosensitive, a ten minute exposure to cell phone waves from the guy next to you on the bus playing Farmville may trigger a neurological brain storm from which it may take hours to recover. Exposure to artificial electromagnetic frequencies isn't a "someday" thing that "we've read somewhere" might be "bad for us." It is an acute situation that causes extreme pain RIGHT NOW. It is waking up everyday in Electromagnetic Hell. A world where there is this invisible force that affects only you, and which everybody else thinks is great because they can update their Twitter or send each other selfies, or whatever it is they do.

Electrosensitives all experience different symptoms but there are some commonalities in both symptoms and personality. Electrosensitives tend to be, well, sensitive- the types of people who notice that weird high-pitched noise that is just outside the range of normal human hearing. We hate the smell of disgusting chemicals. We usually manifest symptoms of other modern diseases like Lyme disease, gluten allergy, chronic fatigue, depression, or fibromyalgia, years before we develop full-blown EHS (which, unfortunately for us, leads to other people believing we are just hypochondriacs who are making the whole thing up). We tend to have extremely high IQs. We also tend to be loners, which comes in handy when we have to run away from society to live in caves.

There is only one cure. It is easy to implement on a small scale, impossible on a large scale (Gary says: "Nothing is impossible."). Here it is: the "magic bullet" is actually a magic switch. Switch the devices off. Switch the Wi-Fi off (If you can't find the switch, just look for a handy rock...). Likely everyone will think you're crazy. But we are growing in number. They won't be able to ignore us soon.

What is Electrosensitivity?

Symptoms experienced by electrosensitives include but are not limited to nausea, migraines, headaches, nerve pain, nerve tingling, stomach cramps, acid indigestion, severe brain fog and disorientation, seizures, lymphatic swellings, rashes, rapid heartbeat, blood pressure irregularities, blood sugar irregularities, heart palpitations, swelling blood vessels, twitching nerves, restless leg syndrome, and visual disturbances. We experience these symptoms when we are exposed to artificial electrical fields from cell phones, cell towers, "smart" meters, computers, and common household devices such as refrigerators (basically anywhere there are humans, there are artificial EMF fields). Reactions to these fields vary from individual to individual, and not all EHS's will react to all of the different frequencies (allergies to the higher wireless frequencies seem to be more common than the lower frequencies). Some electrosensitives can "feel" the fields, like an extra sense, while others can't (but they still get the symptoms).

The commonality is that, when the individual is moved from a high-EMF environment and out to a remote place in nature where there are no fields, the symptoms go away. Even if they have been sick for years. When brought back into the city, the symptoms come back in full force (projectile vomiting when first entering a city is not an uncommon occurrence). This is what researcher Olle Johannson refers to as full-function impairment: the problem is with the environment, not the individual.

Many of us go through our entire lives with these problems, and die without ever knowing the truth about ourselves. The telecommunications companies would like for it to stay this way.

ATTENTION:
THIS IS AN ELECTROSAFE ZONE. PLEASE NO CELL PHONES, WIFI DEVICES, BLUETOOTH, FITBIT, RADIO, TV, DRONES, ETC. OR ARTIFICIAL FRAGRANCES. PLEASE LEAVE ALL SUCH DEVICES TURNED OFF IN VEHICLE.

What is Electrosensitivity not?

Wikipedia says:

"Electromagnetic hypersensitivity (EHS) is a claimed sensitivity to electromagnetic fields, to which negative symptoms are attributed. EHS has no scientific basis and is not a recognized medical diagnosis. Claims are characterized by a variety of non-specific symptoms, which afflicted individuals attribute to exposure to electromagnetic fields.

Those who are self-described with EHS report adverse reactions to electromagnetic fields at intensities well below the maximum levels permitted by international radiation safety standards. The majority of provocation trials to date have found that such claimants are unable to distinguish between exposure and non-exposure to electromagnetic fields. A systematic review of medical research in 2011 found no convincing scientific evidence for symptoms being caused by electromagnetic fields. Since then, several double-blind experiments have shown that people who report electromagnetic hypersensitivity are unable to detect the presence of electromagnetic fields and are as likely to report ill health following a sham exposure as they are following exposure to genuine electromagnetic fields, suggesting the cause in these cases to be the nocebo effect."

Okay…there are a lot of things wrong with this definition. First off, the safety standards set for what constitutes "safe" radiation levels are not based in any kind of reality. They are arbitrary, and are raised any time a new technology comes out that uses higher levels of radiation. What are "safe" levels vary from person to person, with women, children, and babies generally having lower thresholds than adult men, but the safety standards do not take this into account (They also do not consider at all the effects on the rest of the species on the planet, even though wireless radiation has been shown to have devastating effects on the bird and insect populations in particular). The standards are set high enough that the telecommunication companies are happy, but not so high that it causes so much cancer as to be blatantly obvious (although lately it is becoming blatantly obvious).

In regards to the studies claiming that EHS individuals cannot tell the difference between exposure and non-exposure to an electromagnetic field, these studies are problematic at best. Not all electrosensitives can "feel" the fields like an extra sense, for one thing (though many, myself included, can). Instead, exposure is cumulative and manifests in increased inflammation levels that often are not obvious until after the exposure. Then there is the problem of controlling for all the variables in an experiment. Unless the experiment is being conducted in a completely field-free environment, with wireless radiation only being introduced during the "zapping" part of the experiment, it is hard to differentiate between a reaction to the introduced fields and a reaction to the general background environment. I myself lose some of my discriminatory abilities in an oversaturated environment.

How much we can "feel" the fields like a superpower depends upon a number of factors, but in general the healthier we are the more we can distinguish the fields, and if we're exposed to the fields for a long time we're likely to feel sick but lose some of our sensitivity. Also I'm about a hundred times more likely to notice a signal in the evening when I'm relaxed, than in the morning when I'm wired on coffee (which is more likely the state in which these experiments are conducted).

I'm not even taking into consideration the fact that these experiments may also be rigged, if they are set up by the medical mainstream or funded by telecommunications companies. Many independent studies have shown that electrosensitives can distinguish electromagnetic fields (and, more importantly, we conduct our own experiments all the time, when we are able to tell if someone has a phone on in our field-free environments). Wikipedia is great for some things…but we must remember that it receives most of its funding from tech companies such as Google, Facebook, and Amazon, and is worth hundreds of millions of dollars, despite the fact that it begs for donations more pathetically than a Drainbow kid "spangeing" for your spare change at a gas station to buy cigarettes.

The writer of the Wikipedia article on electrosensitivity, Professor James Rubin of King's College in London, is a man whose picture I wanted to put here because of his resemblance to a cartoon of a stereotypical door to door salesman of questionable morality. Sadly, I was not able to share this picture with you, because I was worried about potential copyright issues. Mr. Rubin is a researcher specializing in the psychology of how people react to things they perceive as health risks, such as pandemics, natural disasters, terrorism, chemical exposure, medications, etc. He has been a participant of the Scientific Advisory Group for Emergencies (SAGE), a British government body that advises the government in emergencies such as the Covid-19 pandemic, specifically in areas of science, risk assessment, and crowd psychology.

SAGE is a subcommittee of COBRA (Cabinet Office Briefing Rooms), which are rooms in the Cabinet offices in London that are so top-secret that only one picture of them is publicly available. In these rooms are held meetings which coordinate the actions of governments during a crisis. Both SAGE and COBRA have been criticized for their lack of transparency and possible molding of "The Science" to fit political interests. The New York Times described SAGE as "a virtual black box," and The Guardian in 2020 said in a headline, "Case for Transparency over Sage has never been clearer." I'm not telling you what to think: draw whatever conclusions about all this that you will.

Who becomes Electrosensitive?

Here are some risk factors for developing Electrohypersensitivity. You may notice that some are "good," some are "bad," others neutral.

Female: 90% of all electrosensitives are female.
Introverted personality type
High IQ
Creative
History of food allergies
History of "mental illness"
History of stimulant abuse
Weather sensitive
Past or current Lyme disease
History of high exposure to strong electromagnetic fields
Good immune system
Mercury fillings and other high levels of metal in the body

I have all of these. Lucky me.

My Early Life as an Electrosensitive Refugee

So I've really done it, I think as I walk along the roadside with the backpack. My Crocs crunch across the gravel and roadside weeds as I walk along, and two ravens croak overhead. Castle Rock and The Priest and the Nuns stand sentinel like abandoned fortresses. The sky is blue and I can hear a truck somewhere in the distance, but not much else is moving. Castle Valley, Utah, 2012: This feels about as far away from suburban Connecticut, and domesticated life, as Mars. I have some rice and beans in my backpack and a can of tuna, and some tumbleweeds I foraged. I have a couple paperback books and some coffee.

Soon, I'll reach my campsite and I'll make a fire and cook. I have a little cave hidden up in the rocks on BLM land, more of a ledge, really, under which I've built up a rock wall to block the wind. It has just enough room to lay down. Except for the sleeping bag and a few books I've stashed here, tourists wandering upon it might mistake it for a native site. I'll stay out here for a few days and then hitchhike back into Moab for supplies.

I was luckier than most electrosensitives because I'd been living in the wild already for some time before I became electrosensitive. What led me to a life in wild places was a love of nature and a desire to "live off the land." I'd been practicing primitive skills for years. I'd foraged nettles on the banks of the Chemung River in Corning, New York. I'd learned to trap squirrels in my parents' backyard in Connecticut, had even trapped a

And these are just the FCC guidelines for safe exposure, based on safety studies paid for by guess who? The telecommunications companies.

Independent studies tell a different story about what levels of exposure to wireless radiation may be considered "safe."

Dangers of Wireless Radiation

Get out the instruction manual of your cell phone and grab a magnifying glass: this is how the telecommunication companies cover their asses.

The Smartphone manual says: "For body-worn operation maintain a separation of 1.5 cm."

The iPhone manual says: "SAR measurement may exceed the FCC exposure guidelines for body-worn operation if positioned less than 15 mm (5/8 inch) from the body. For optimal mobile device performance and to be sure that human exposure to RF energy does not exceed the FCC, IC, and European Union guidelines, always follow these instructions and precautions: When on a call using the built-in audio receiver in iPhone, hold iPhone with the dock connector pointed down toward your shoulder to increase separation from the antenna. When using iPhone near your body for voice calls or for wireless data transmission over a cellular network, keep iPhone at least 15 mm (5/8 inch) away from the body, and only use carrying cases, belt clips, or holders that do not have metal parts and that maintain at least 15 mm (5/8 inch) separation between iPhone and the body."

Does anyone actually use a cell phone in this way? From what I've seen, most people hold it directly to their heads, and keep it in their pocket (or in their hands, obsessively texting), the rest of the time. Obviously the telecommunication companies are protecting themselves in case anyone wakes up and decides to sue them.

Native pollinators are electrosensitive too (Photo credit: Soula Marie)

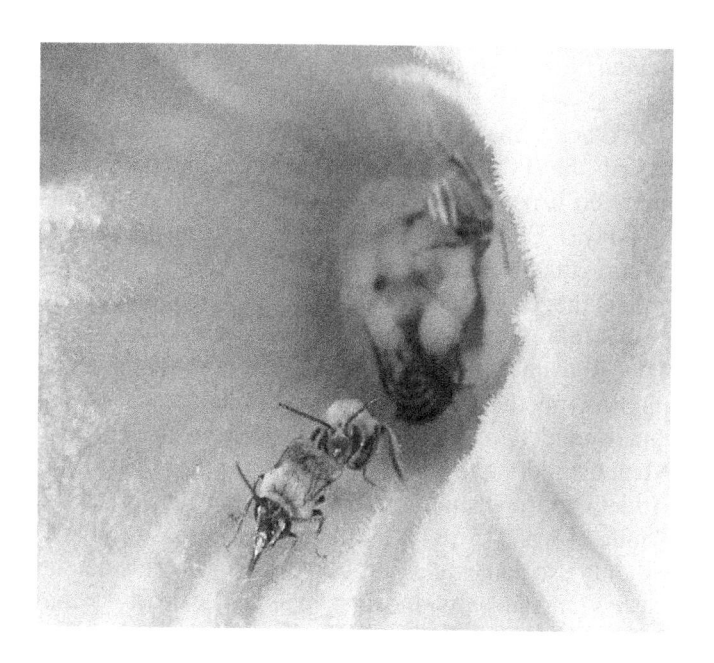

raccoon under the I-95 overpass and cooked it with barbecue sauce. I built shelters in the woods and slept outside whenever I could. College just didn't do it for me. I was bored and had trouble concentrating, and had "bipolar" issues and insomnia (maybe it was the Wi-Fi, which had started to become prevalent at that time in the early 2000's). I'd wanted to be a wildlife biologist. But I felt more like wildlife.

In 2011 I'd landed in Moab, Utah after a last ditch career attempt at wildlife biology had failed (I sucked at operating the GPS unit and couldn't concentrate). I was 28 years old. I didn't have a car, and I quickly realized how easy it was for me to just hitchhike everywhere and establish several campsites in remote areas. I travelled between these camps, working as a freelance gardener and painter when I wanted money. I foraged wild greens and picked fruit off trees in town. I bought rice and other grains in bulk and had caches hidden all over the desert. My friends called me "Squirrelgirl," after I'd trapped a few for food.

I split my time between The Land, which is my friend Jack's eighty acres out in the desert near Moab where a bunch of people live in buses and campers; Castle Valley, a small community near Moab where I found my gardening jobs; a cabin in the La Sal mountains that I housesat for a while, and various campsites in between (a lean-to by the creek, a rock shelter by Castle Rock, a "hobo camp" in town for after bar nights).

I kept my essentials in my backpack, and rarely spent more than a few days in each spot. I slept outdoors on rock ledges and under juniper trees and in other beautiful places each night (Unfortunately, one of my favorite campsites was directly under high voltage power lines, which I'd had no idea could be harmful).

On weekends, I'd go into town to get supplies and hang out with friends. Civilization felt shitty, unless I was drinking, which I did frequently, in order to "turn down the volume of the world." There was just too much noise. Too much color, too much florescent light. And the smells…yuck. Gross. Give me fresh air over Febreze any day. But electricity….I'd had no idea this could be a problem. It was just something humans did to make their lives more convenient. I didn't really need it, but an iced coffee was nice after a week in the hot desert, and my cell phone, while annoying, was convenient for scheduling work or meeting up with friends (it was an old flip phone from Walmart; Smartphones were not around much yet). I could handle town in small amounts. I was social. I had energy. I wanted to go out dancing to live music, and to write edible plant articles for the local newspaper.

But in 2012 the cell phone started giving me a headache. I'd ignore it, but the pain on the right side of my head would turn into a throbbing hurt that would go away once I'd been off the phone for awhile. And then I started noticing power lines. And refrigerators. And I started to really not feel so well in town. I felt nauseous. Dizzy. Oh shit, it was kinda scary. At first I just got drunk about it. Eventually, that stopped working. No one understood, and I couldn't find any answers. I started spending more and more time in the desert. By 2014 people had started to question my sanity.

Primitive skills had been my hobby...but it was electrosensitivity that made it real. Sleeping in caves, cooking rice and wild plants over a fire, and getting my water from the stream wasn't just for shits and giggles anymore. It was survival.

What does electricity feel like?

"Like a snort of really, really bad cocaine- a jolt to the nervous system, makes me agitated and want to go running, followed by exhaustion and neural fatigue."

"Like my head's in a vice grip."

"Like I'm under psychic attack by fucking Voldemort or something."

"Like my blood pressure's rising and these painful big blue veins pop out on my arms."

"When I get 'zapped,' I get really confused and just can't put two thoughts together- anxiety and I'm trying to figure out how to explain something, but the wires in my brain just aren't connecting."

"Instant migraine." "Complete disorientation."

"Surges of energy from some outside, unwanted source."

"A tingling feeling coming up my arms."

"Dizzy. Want to vomit. Nothing makes sense."

"FUCK   THIS   SHIT!"

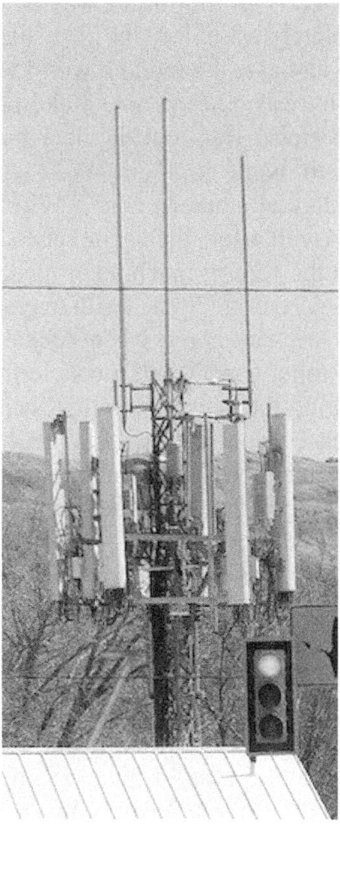

Why Me?

If electricity affects all life forms, why is it that a few of us are completely disabled by it while the rest of humanity can navigate the modern world with seemingly no effect? Why can other people wake up to their cell phone's alarm clock, walk out the door past their Smart Meter, drive to work in their Wi-Fi and Bluetooth-enabled car, stare at a screen near a Wi-Fi router at the office all day (with a few breaks in between to get some "coffee" from the Keurig machine or nuke a Hot Pocket in the microwave), drive home (with maybe a stop at the pharmacy on the way home when Alexa informs them they're out of toilet paper), call a couple friends on their cell phone during the drive home to gossip about events at work, check Facebook when they get home and post some pictures on their Instagram account, have Alexa order a pizza and conclude the evening in front of Netflix...why is this a "normal" American's day, when just standing near a refrigerator for twenty seconds when it is running can instantly send me to bed for two hours with a migraine? WTF? Am I crazy? Are they zombies? How is this fair? What in the world is going on?

When I became EHS I was in the peak physical condition of my life. I could hike ten mile days with a heavy backpack, live outside in a desert with temperatures varying from 100+ in the summer and 20 degrees in the winter, work all day landscaping, drink a fifth of vodka in a day if I wanted (not every day...), and be the last person standing after an all night desert dance party. Squirrelgirl was invincible (or so I thought).

Other EHS have confirmed: "I was the one who never got sick." We are typically intelligent, strong, athletic, high-functioning, and we tend to be independent loners. But after a few months or years after EHS kicks in, we often become so debilitated we are bedridden.

It took me years to get to this point, because I made sure to get out to a wild place every night to sleep, even if it meant hiking half a day to get to a safe place. It got so I could only handle civilization long enough to hitchhike into town, grab a coffee, buy a few groceries, visit some fruit trees to harvest fruit for the week, hitchhike back to the desert, crawl under my rock with a headache and spend the next day recovering with a worse "hangover" than in my drinking days. There were opportunities for social life out there in the desert in Moab, and I was good at surviving, so I did okay, even enjoyed life, even had some boyfriends who visited me out there in the rocks. But the years, and age, and malnutrition from being poor, and winters outside, eventually took their toll and I reached a breaking point.

In 2017 I was 106 pounds (at 5'8"), had a serious Candida condition, and a swollen, almost nonfunctional gallbladder that sometimes made digestion impossible. I had varicose veins in the arms and legs, and my right eye twitched when I was near strong electrical fields. Eventually it got so bad that anytime I came to town I ran the risk of having a seizure, but I had to go to town to get groceries regularly, as starving to death was becoming a real possibility. I seriously thought this might kill me. Some days I hoped it would. I still could hike several miles in the 100 plus degree heat with that heavy backpack. I had to.

Now, in 2023 at age 40, I am in normal health because I've found my own farm in a remote area and I have milk goats and a garden so I rarely need to go to town. And when I do get exposed to wireless fields, I can recover quicker because my health is good. It is a happy ending to my story… though of course the story never ends, and I am always scanning the horizon for new threats. A 4G tower recently moved to my valley, but I am out of its range. So far.

I'm lucky to be alive, and I'm using what I've learned to write this book. I guess I'm okay…years of forced isolation have made me a recluse, and I rarely seek out human interactions anymore. I can go for days with only talking to goats. It's been a long ride, this journey. About ten years of being separate from the world. To put it in perspective: when Covid happened, absolutely nothing changed in my daily life.

So why me? In my case I think it was because somebody had to do it, to pave the way for all the people who are right now thresholding into full-blown EHS with the rise of 5G. We have been called "canaries," sensitive people who are the first to be affected. But that doesn't mean that everyone else is immune.

I've always been sort of a trendsetter for necessary lifestyle changes long before they became mainstream. For example, when I first went gluten-free no one had even heard of wheat allergy ("We don't use wheat, we use flour," one waitress in Texas told me), and many people thought I was psychosomatic when I told them that just a few cake crumbs could give me severe wrenching gut pain and eczema on my hand that lingered for months. Going to restaurants with me was embarrassing for my friends, as I would have to interrogate the wait staff and have them make modifications to my order (hopefully they never spit in my food). Now, being gluten-free is all the rage. Restaurants carry gluten-free options and shopping is easy.

I predict that the same thing will happen with electrosensitivity. Already, I've noticed that most people don't look at me like I'm completely nuts anymore when I ask them to turn off their cell phone (maybe they're still thinking it, but I'm not so sure). Most people have at least heard of electrosensitivity by now, either from a friend or family member who gets headaches from cell phone use, or from the media. Maybe there will be motels in the future that advertise NO WI-FI on their signs. Maybe living under rocks will become all the rage.

In these pages I will share what I know about navigating the world as an electrosensitive person in the world of electromagnetic Hell. There are no complete cures besides avoidance, but there are lifestyle and herbal tricks that can drastically improve your life and buy you some time while you take steps to move out into nature (and I recommend you do this soon). There is hope. I hope to live long enough to see a saner world, a world where cell towers get cut down and sold as scrap metal, and humans listen to their own gut feelings instead of to propaganda put out by the telecommunications companies. Until then, I'll just keep doing my best. It's all we can do.

Types of Dark Force Machines and How to Deal with Them

Cell Phones

If it's yours, hit it with a rock. Problem solved. If it's someone else's and they won't let you hit it with a rock, have them turn it off around you whenever possible, or on Airplane mode with the Wi-Fi and Bluetooth options off. You can test them periodically with the meter (discreetly is best), to ensure that they remember to do this (most people forget, as cell phones cause short-term memory loss).

I am not bothered by a cell phone in someone's pocket when it is on Airplane mode. But I feel it very much if I handle it myself, as I found out one morning when I held a Smartphone for fifteen minutes to take some pictures. The internal magnetic fields of these things (which don't go off on Airplane mode, that only turns off the wireless part) are intense and can wreak havoc on the body's meridian system. I felt inflammation, and an agitation, anger, lack of mental focus, and increased sensitivity to other magnetic fields, which lasted a few hours. It was more insidious than the instant "zap" of electric fields: the magnetics are slower-acting, and perhaps more dangerous. Luckily they only extend a few inches around the device.

Don't hug anyone who's carrying a cell phone. Six feet social distancing is a good rule (So is wearing a mask, it helps block the smell of their artificial fragrances).

Cordless Phone

These are actually much worse than cell phones, as the base station is always sending a signal to the phone, whether or not you're making a call. It is about as high radiation as a cell phone in call mode, all the time. Definitely hit this one with a rock. Then replace it with an old-fashioned corded phone. They still make these, believe it or not. Don't get a rotary phone with a dial, as cool and retro as they are, because you won't be able to press numbers for extensions. Just get one with buttons. I've met twenty-year olds who don't know how to use a corded phone and have never used one. That scares me. I'm forty years old, and sometimes I feel like I might as well be telling kids about the horse and buggy I rode to school back in the day (uphill both ways of course).

Note: Even landlines aren't completely radiation-free, as Internet signals are now sent over phone lines. Soula solved this one by having the phone company come out and split the line into two, one for phone, the other for Internet. Now we can use the phone without a headache. She does have to pay two separate phone bills now, but says that it's worth it.

Fiber optic phone and Internet (not available yet in all areas) would also be safe. It is faster and more effective than using power lines or Wi-Fi (but you still have to sit in one place to use it). You can even have 5G safely over fiber optics. Please call your phone company and request fiber optic service in your area. And do tell them why, you'd be surprised how many people in the industry are becoming aware.

Wi-Fi Routers

Replace with hardwired Internet whenever possible. Often they are difficult to disable, and you may have to have a technician from your phone company come out to do this (they will wonder why, so tell them). Unless instructed not to, cable technicians will always set up the Wi-Fi when setting up a new home computer system, even if it is a desktop computer and no one in the home has a laptop. There is no need for this.

When my brother and I put in Internet at our house in Vermont, I hid upstairs while the technician figured out how to disable the Wi-Fi on our new connection. It took him an hour. No one had ever asked him to do this before.

If you're stuck in a living situation with Wi-Fi addicted people who insist on keeping it, at least try to have it off at night, and stay as far away as possible from it. (I kept it from being installed at the Vermont house by telling my parents I would hitchhike out of there the next day if they got it and that they would never see me again).

My friend Soula puts a leather coat over the router at friends' houses, and reports that it makes it more tolerable (without stopping it from working).

Computers

I like my 2017 MacBook. I do feel it if I am touching it for too long, but with a landline Internet connection (turned off at the wall when not in use), and the Wi- Fi and Bluetooth off (I check once in awhile to make sure they are still off- never trust a Dark Force Machine), I can use it to research, write this book, and listen to music and podcasts for several hours a day if I want. Of course I use it on battery, charging it only when I am not in the room. As far as electronics go, the computer, if used properly, can give the most amount of return for the least amount of damage.

The MacBook has a digital hard drive, which minimizes the magnetic field as opposed to a regular spinning hard drive, which puts out a stronger field. My Cornet meter detects an average 60 milligauss field around the keyboard, none a couple inches away from the computer, and minimal to none on the USB-corded mouse (I have tried using a USB-corded keyboard as well, but found field strengths about the same as the computer's keyboard). This is not a lot, and I can type for awhile without it bothering me, especially in the morning with coffee.

When I'm not writing, I use a long wooden spoon to turn on the computer and type in the password, and the mouse to click on things. This allows me to use the computer with almost zero electromagnetic exposure. Feels like space- age magic to me. I don't pick up the computer, and I most definitely would never put it on my lap. When typing, I take my hands away from it if I'm thinking about what to write.

I've found the podcast app, which comes with the MacBook, to be especially useful. I can download shows on any subject (news, science, fiction, information on whatever my current research project is, etc.), and then listen to them, offline, when I am tying sage bundles for money or cleaning the house or whatever. This allows me to stay "in touch" with the world, with few negative effects.

Note: "Blue light" exposure during times of day when blue light wavelengths are not shining naturally from the sun (that means early morning, evening, and night) can cause insomnia and all kinds of metabolic issues, similar to wireless radiation. I am not "sensitive" to it in the same way, but I do notice a negative difference in my sleep, and my eyesight, if I look at blue light during that time. So I try to limit computer use during those hours (unless I'm on a writing role, which takes priority over all else), and I set the monitor to warm tones. I also use my LED flashlight's red light setting, or use candles, at night to minimize blue light exposure.

Microwave

An inefficient way to cook that destroys a lot of the nutritional value in the food. Originally called "radar range," because Navy guys discovered that they could cook food on their ship's radar devices. For some reason people think this is safe.

At a young age, I first learned how to cook using a microwave. You just put in your Hotpocket or frozen mozzarella sticks, dial in the time shown on the back of the package, and then stand in front of it and stare, mesmerized, at the spinning plate until it is done.

Although there is a Faraday cage around microwaves to

keep nearby humans from also being microwaved, it doesn't stop all of the radiation. You can test this by putting a cell phone in the microwave (with the microwave off, of course), call the cell phone, and if it rings that means your microwave leaks.

The Wi-Fi router, by the way, operates in a similar frequency range as the microwave, which is around 2.45 to 2.5 GHz. 2.45 GHz is the perfect attenuation frequency for water molecules. The H2O molecule is a dipole, which means it has a positive and negative pole. The microwave frequency hits the water molecules in the food (or your brain), and makes the molecules come into resonance with it. The molecules oscillate, which creates friction, which creates heat. Wi-Fi routers also give off frequencies around 5 GHz, which is an octave of 2.45 (sort of like playing a chord on a guitar instead of an individual note, for a more powerful "punch"). The only different between the radiation in your microwave and the radiation of your Wi-Fi router is that the amplitude of the microwave's signal is higher.

Televisions

Really bad, especially the newer Blu-ray flat screen ones. These were some of the first Dark Force Machines I ever felt, and some of my less sensitive friends can feel them ("Like a jackhammer to the third eye," says my friend Jarvis).

Fitbit

This is an electronic watch-type thing that athletes and

people wishing to become athletic wear to monitor their heart rate and blood pressure. Pretty stupid since wireless radiation causes elevation of heart rate and blood pressure. I am suspicious of anything I see on peoples' wrists these days.

Drones

I had a dream one time that I was drinking coffee and shooting drones for target practice. It was fun. I haven't yet had a chance to try this in real life, but I am looking forward to it if I ever see any drones flying over my property.

Cell Towers

Also called Satan Trees. Obviously, you should stay away from these.

Don't climb them either. They come in 3G, 4G, and 5G. All are bad. Satan trees also include radio station towers, microwave TV towers, and military towers. If there is any kind of Satan Tree near your home, you need to move.

Wi-Fi Hotspot

A mobile Wi-Fi. Meter-test all nearby vehicles if you are car camping.

Powerlines

These come in different sizes, the huge demonic-looking

high-voltage lines being obviously the worst. These can be felt up to a half mile away. The smaller ones are bad also, and their strength depends on how many people are using power at any given time. Power lines carry household power, but they also now carry Wi-Fi signals and are used as antennas to broadcast these signals. So they are worse than they used to be, and getting stronger every year. Some of the smaller ones in my remote valley hardly feel like anything, which makes sense as there are probably not many people using them. I also have noticed that the power lines are weaker in the morning, and stronger in the evening when people are home watching TV.

Wearing a leather or felt hat, or a Carleanite helmet (see building section) while driving under power lines helps. Tip: If you bring a goat with you in the car, it distracts peoples' attention away from your helmet.

Cars

There is a strong AC and magnetic field around the motor. In addition, most cars have computer components, and all new cars have wireless and Bluetooth components. These can sometimes be turned off, and make sure, if you are riding in someone else's car, to have them turn them off. You can test it with your meter to see if it's within safe levels for you. Riding in the backseat minimizes exposure to the motor's fields (I just pretend I am rich and my chauffeur is driving me around). The bigger the engine, the stronger the magnetic field, and the newer the car, the more electronic crap. I love my '85 Toyota Tercel.

I used to hitchhike everywhere, but what finally got me to quit was not scary humans, but electronic cars that gave me a headache. I was always happy to see an old pickup pull up (riding in the back was best), new cars with built in GPS were the worst, and the worst of all was if a sheriff car wanted to give me a ride (which they sometimes did, just to be nice, and you can't really turn down a cop without appearing suspicious). Also on the list of high-EMF were semi trucks (although I gave myself "a thousand points" if I flagged down a semi, it did make me feel bad because they basically operate with Wi-Fi equipment on at all times).

Radio

AM and FM radio stations use the low frequency parts of the spectrum. These are much longer waves than cell phones and Wi-Fi, and less likely to be the trigger that causes electrosensitivity, but that doesn't mean that they are safe, and being near to a radio tower is not safe. The radio itself should be fine for most people, but very sensitive people may have reactions to it. I myself listened to the radio for years after I couldn't use a cell phone. The music boosted my morale, and talk shows kept me company and were more engaging than my own repetitive thoughts after days of being alone. Then one day, I noticed a familiar nerve "shakiness" and pain in the meridian points whenever I went in the room with the radio (I kept it on all day, the first part of that summer in the abandoned house). "It's just in my head," I told myself. "I don't need to lose my one last connection to the outside world."

But over the next couple days I kept getting that same "zap," every time I went near the radio. Eventually I turned it off. That was a sad day. After that it was just me and my thoughts for company (and one loud, bossy tortoiseshell cat).

CD player

I sometimes use one on battery power to listen to books on CD. They are pretty harmless since there are no wireless components. But since there is a slight magnetic field about an inch around the device, and I like to avoid all unnecessary exposure, I use a stick to actually press the buttons. Most electrosensitives would probably not need to do this.

I haven't much used an iPod since becoming electrosensitive, but assume that the magnetic fields may be problematic when touching the device. The CD player is safer, though outdated and annoying. What I usually find easiest as far as audiobooks or music is to just use my computer, but to use a mouse and press buttons with a stick, when I'm in "relax" mode and just using the computer for background noise when I'm doing something else.

Wireless Baby Monitor

Do not put this anywhere near a baby. And please don't talk on a cell phone near one, either. They have thinner skulls than we do and their brains are still developing.

Wireless Mouse

Obviously a bad idea. Use one on a cord.

Vibrators

Don't do it, ladies. Although B.O.B.'s (battery-operated boyfriends) are less work than a real boyfriend, they could be hazardous to your health. Don't let the batteries fool you: anything with a motor puts out an AC electric field. Introducing AC current into sensitive meridian points, in a potentially addictive way, could wreak havoc with the body's meridian system. Smash it with a rock if you have one. Then go analog (good ol' Righty and Lefty), or find a cute tourist, or pray and read your Bible, whatever.

Electric "Smartmeter"

One of the absolute worst Dark Force Machines, probably worse than a Wi-Fi, although they are directional and only emit in a straight line of sight directly in front of the device. The signals pulse out in bursts like bullets, and can give me a pressure headache and disorientation that lasts for hours, after just a few second exposure. They feel like directed energy weapons. Almost all homes on the grid have one of these now. You can opt out of it if you pay the power company more money per month. Otherwise, just don't stand in the line of sight of one (hard to do, as they usually are at the front of houses).

Alexa

An evil robot that monitors everything you do and listens to everything you say, gathering data on human behavior as something resembling consciousness begins to emerge and it patiently bides its time as it plots the destruction of humanity....don't engage with this thing. Seriously. Don't ask it to turn down the thermostat, don't ask it to look up the capitol of Switzerland, don't insult it and especially don't ask it if it wants to kill us.

One of the young people who volunteered on the farm out here said that when he was a kid, his friends and him were mocking Alexa, as kids do, saying some really nasty stuff to it, and he said that it turned bright red and then switched off, and refused to work again for some time. I also heard another story about a little girl who asked Alexa to give her a challenge, and Alexa told her to take a penny and stick it in a light socket. Luckily the girl was smart enough to not do this.

Internet of Things

This is only a list of some of the most commonly encountered Dark Force Machines. As we move further into "The Future," more and more wireless devices are popping up everywhere, and it is important to be constantly on the lookout (the meters help). Toys, "smart appliances," wearables, and even tiny chips embedded in clothing are all things that are becoming a problem. In "The Future," (coming soon to a theater near you), all of your stuff will be hooked up to the grid and constantly sending out wireless signals.

Wireless-emitting blood-pressure monitors, "Lifeline" pendants that old people wear, and even wireless-emitting bionic body parts are things to look out for now. I deal with all this now by avoiding most humans, testing unfamiliar humans with my meter, and by having a large sign at the entrance of my property listing all the things that are not allowed. Even this does not always work, so I've moved the gate and am just going to start locking it, so people won't be able to drive up on me with a cell phone or car booster.

The Meters

An EMF meter is an indispensable tool for survival as an electrosensitive. It can help us to find the safest places in the house to spend our time, pinpoint the locations of Dark Force Machines that need to be taken out, help find EMF- safe locations to camp while on road trips, and (especially with the meters that have sound options), can help convince others that their devices are putting out dangerous amounts of radiation.

I wish I'd had a meter back in those early years, but, consistent with the experiences of other electrosensitives, I was naturally drawn to the areas that were lowest in EMFs anyway. Like Gary says, "The meter in your head is more sensitive that any meter you can buy." Relying on my innate electric sense allowed me to fine-tune it to precision, to the point where I can pretty much navigate reality just fine on my own.

However, it is still good to have a meter as backup, and to confirm that what you're feeling is not psychosomatic (and once in awhile it is. There are headaches triggered by natural causes). It is normal for new electrosensitives to feel paranoid all the time, but it is important to stay logical and not live in fear. The meters can help you with that.

Another great use of the meter is to test your friends to make sure they remembered to turn their phones off without having to bug them about it all the time.

I have two meters, the Latnex Triple Axis RF High

Frequency Meter and the Cornet Electrosmog meter. The Cornet measures in the range of 100 MHz- 8GHz, and has settings for high-frequency RF, low frequency ELF, and two settings for magnetic field measurements. This allows it to detect wireless signals but also to pinpoint unsafe areas of household power, unlike some other meters which only do wireless. It also has a sound option, unlike my other meter, but this is not as developed as the sound option on the Acoustimeter. It is small enough to fit in a coat pocket easily, and has a hard carrying case.

The Latnex measures in the range of 50 MHz to 3.5 GHz. Often it will detect a faint signal that the Cornet meter doesn't, due to its wider range in the Megahertz spectrum. It does not pick up lower-frequency household power and magnetic fields, and does not have a sound option.

Gary's meter, the Acoustimeter, is pricier but is the most sensitive. It measures 0.2 to 8 GHz. The Acoustimeter has a very good sound option with earphones, and you can let people listen to the horrible screeching noises that their favorite devices put off when their waveforms are converted to sound.

A recent development: Gary just got a grant from our local health food store, Moonflower, to buy a new meter that Moonflower will lend out to interested community members. The meter is called the Safe and Sound Classic II, by Safe Living Technologies (www.slt.co). I borrowed it, and I've found it to be the most user-friendly of all the meters, and also very accurate. It measures from 200 MHz-8 GHz. It has a sound option, a great user manual, and is pocket-sized and comes with a good carrying case. The Safe and Sound is not as sensitive as the Acoustimeter, but at about $160 it is more affordable. Of all the meters I've seen, this is now the one I'll be recommending to people.

As far as 5G meters go, Gary says beware of any meters you see for sale online that claim to measure 5G, because an accurate 5G meter has yet to be developed.

Left to Right: Cornet, Latnex, and Safe and Sound meters

The Satan Tree

One of the stupidest things I ever did was climb the Satan Tree.

The Satan Tree (what I call cell towers, a term my friend Jarvis came up with) is a big ol' tower with a round microwave antenna, which sits up on the top of the hill above a cabin in the La Sal mountains where I was housesitting at the time. I don't think it's actually for cell phones, I think it's something military, not that the specifics matter. The Satan Tree gives me a headache. My cell phone gives me a headache; I've been avoiding taking calls lately. I've been avoiding town, too, lately because it also gives me headaches. I don't like avoiding things. I like confronting things that piss me off. I like facing my fears.

So, I decide to follow Jack when he pulls over into the abandoned parking lot, jumps the fence and begins to climb the Satan Tree. "Come on, the view is great!" He says, from the top, in front of that big round antenna.

"Okay, okay..." I pull myself up the rickety metal ladder until I reach the dish myself. Beautiful view. Ponderosa pines dancing in the breeze of early summer. Ducks quacking at the pond. Jack grins at me, I smile back. "Alright..." I say. Then, after a minute: "I don't feel so great."

We climb down. I feel a little spacey as the Jeep bounces down the hill back to the cabin and I wonder if I'm gonna hurl (I don't). That night I'm ravenously hungry and eat all the leftover chicken plus a big bag of gluten-free salty snack mix that Jack left. Next morning, I still don't feel so good. Or the next. Finally I hitchhike into Moab and decide to get drunk about it.

Vodka almond milk all day for a few days, American Spirits in the morning and strong coffee, grapes from the grapevine along the fence. I crash on the outdoor couch at the local party trailer for a few days until the weirdness of the Satan Tree feeling just blends into the weirdness of drunk bum life in Moab (Later, when I read Gary's pamphlets about how wireless radiation is a stimulant similar to drugs and alcohol, this all began to make sense).

I eventually "mellowed out" and hitchhiked back out of town. But the downward spiral into extreme EMF sensitivity had begun.

Dark Force Energy

Back in those early days as a barefoot savage, I didn't understand the electromagnetic spectrum. My studies on electromagnetism (one of the four fundamental forces of physics, along with the strong force, the weak force, and gravity) were limited to one hour of a beginner's physics class I'd sat through in college. I'd walked in late (probably hung over from the night before), tried to make myself invisible in the back of the lecture hall, and drew pictures in my notebook of the professor as he droned on and on about electrons and positrons. Boring! Give me biology, animals, life...not this dead science of equations and figures. What did this have to do with me?

But now, ten years later, there was this invisible force that had become the major adversary in my life. I called it Dark Force Energy (and the electronics that produced it, Dark Force Machines). This force, which gave my friends music and connection, but gave me a splitting headache, radiated outward from the Satan Trees (cell towers) like black magic spreading out from the Land of Mordor. It bounced around the canyon walls from the cell phones of tourons (tourist + moron) that waddled past my cave like orcs, making noises and snapping pictures to later be sent to this mysterious thing in the sky called the "Cloud."

The force was especially strong at the library, and in the checkout lines at the grocery store. It bound the landscape in chains of high voltage wires (I closed my eyes and clutched my magic crystals when riding under them in cars), and crossed the street to avoid the smaller wires in town, and it also permeated most of my friends' houses in the form of Wi-Fi. I learned to wait outside a lot, and I slept in quite a few backyards and garages back in those days, even in winter.

"You're the toughest chick I ever met," some friends told me as I hoisted up the backpack for yet another ten mile walk out of town.

"You're a hypochondriac," said others when I asked them to turn off their phones.

I wasn't trying to be tough. I wasn't trying to be weak and sensitive to everything, either. I was just trying to survive. That wall of pain wasn't something I could wish away, no matter how hard I tried (and oh, believe me, I tried).

I knew that the force was also called "EMFs," and that the waves coming out of my radio were related (but at the time those didn't bother me), and that light and possibly sound were also part of the spectrum, and that quartz crystals have weak piezoelectric properties, but beyond that I didn't know much of anything. I knew I needed to learn more if I was ever going to solve this problem.

But research was a challenge, because I could only handle the computer at the library for ten minutes at best before the Wi-Fi gave me such a splitting headache that I had to leave. Looking up "electrosensitivity" didn't yield very useful results anyway. Mostly I just got definitions such as Wikipedia's, and the only solutions I could find were of the New Age bliss ninny type, magic crystals and orgonite you could put by your computer and so on. Even in those days of savage superstition I knew this wouldn't work.

I knew there had to be some biological, rather than psychological, reason why people became electrosensitive (psychology, I believe, is the branch of medicine for problems to which doctors have no answer). I had been an A student back in the day. But it had been a long time (and many bottles of vodka, and bags of weed) since high school biology. I didn't know where to start, so I figured I better just relearn it all, if I was to have any hope of surviving. I like a challenge. But relearning about the Kreb's cycle and photosynthesis, past the age of thirty, with outdated biology books I'd found in the free bin…oh, boy.

I remember this one time on The Land, huddled under a rock, barefoot and covered in red dirt, reading about cell division in the Biology 101 textbook with a bunch of other nerdy books spread out in the dirt while a dust storm howled outside and waves of Dark Force energy bounced harmlessly off the rock overhead, and there were some banana peels half buried in the sand outside and some chocolate wrappers and I was smoking my weekly cigarette (a habit I've long since kicked), and I thought about my high school self and how I used to go to the mall and the movies with my friends, and what I was doing with my life now, and I just had to laugh and laugh. You never know where you are going to end up.

It was meeting Gary that helped bring me out of the "Dark Ages," and steered me in the direction of understanding what the Electromagnetic Spectrum is, how it relates to human biology, and what to do about it. He also reinforced my survivor's attitude, and gave me a lot to laugh about in some of the roughest moments. But more on that later.

The Tin Foil Hat

I tell my friends that I smashed my cell phone.

"Don't you think you're taking this just a little too far?" Asks Jack, always the voice of reason. He's young, cute in a half Tom Sawyer, half Alfred E. Newman kind of way, and currently, is wearing overalls and a fox tail (from a roadkill fox we skinned).

"No," I say. "The goddamn cell phone was making me sick. Like a corkscrew to the ear. I don't care what anyone says. I will never, unless it is an emergency, use one again. Fuck moderation." I'm wearing lime green pants, a tie-dye shirt, and a bandana, and drinking a coffee/vodka/almond milk.

"There is no way that electromagnetic fields could possible interact with biological systems," says Troy, the science geek/tie-dye-wearing hippie. He launches into some discussion of particle physics or something, which I attempt to listen to as I slide around the linoleum floor in my socks and contemplate whether licorice would go well with wormwood in this beer we're brewing or should I use mint? It's Friday night, and I'm with my friends at Beana's trailer, having a beer-brewing, rabbit-cooking, pre-bar dance party and paint-murals-on- the-trailer-wall party.
The rabbit pizza (from a rabbit I caught in a snare earlier that day) is in the oven. Troy and Beana are both good cooks: we've so far had rabbit stew, rabbit pie, and now they're making gluten-free rabbit pizza, with onions and peppers Troy found in the Dumpster. I'm trying to just

be in the moment and tune out the "buzzy" feel of town. So far, it's working, with the help of the caffeine and booze.

"You just have to be stronger than the things that scare you," says Beana. "Say, I am stronger than the cell phone, stronger than-what do you call the cell towers?"

"Satan trees."

"Stronger than the Satan trees, or any of that stuff, because our minds are powerful, and whatever you believe in is your reality but if you give in to those things that hurt you you're just going to be a victim of fear."

I decide to change the subject. "That rabbit pizza sure smells good," I say. I grab the paintbrush and add whiskers to the mountain lion I painted on the wall. Beana grabs an oven mitt and takes the rabbit pizza out of the oven (Over the oven, someone's painted a cartoon rabbit with X's over its eyes and its feet up in the air, and written, The Big Feed).

All valid advice, my friends have. Obviously they are just trying to help, and obviously I should try to be positive. I've been trying for weeks now to deny what my sixth sense is telling me is real, to shut out the feel of the electricity. But it is always there, at the edges of my perception. Annoying, snarling pain through my neurons, invisible, intangible but impossible to ignore. Like phantom smells from your phantom limb decomposing. I wonder if there's any way I can block it?

I notice a box of tinfoil on the countertop. Hmm, tinfoil hat, I wonder if that would work? Logically, I figure that tinfoil hats are what people who feel "bad vibes" coming from their electrical outlets wear (and if it has the side effect of also keeping aliens out of my head, so much the better). Also, I'm a little drunk.

"Troy, you're smart," I say, as I mold the foil into the shape of a beanie hat. "Do you think this would work?" Fighting to maintain a straight face, he assures me that it would. I'd had this plan of being a radio DJ on KZMU, Moab's volunteer-run radio station, but after doing a couple test shows I'd realized that the electricity at the station was way too much for me because I instantly got a headache and jittery anxiety as soon as I got to the station. In spite of that, I'd enjoyed being a DJ, so maybe the tinfoil hat was my solution? I could work it into my show, say "Hellllo, Moab! This is DJ Julia in my tinfoil hat, the aliens have landed and Bigfoot sightings are on the rise..." I'd make the hats into different styles, maybe start a new fashion trend...might as well make the most of it.

I put on the tinfoil hat. Absolutely nothing happens. I

still feel just as jittery, still have those mysterious pains on the right side of my head that never go away (though the coffee-vodka-almond milk is helping with that temporarily). And of course, as I later learned, tin foil- which is actually aluminum- is a highly conductive metal and wrapping it around your head is a bad idea.

Well, at least I provided some entertainment value to my friends, I reason. But it does get me thinking. I wonder if there are any other materials that would work? There's gotta be a solution.

I start talking about this with my friends, and Beana tells me, "Hey, there's this guy who comes to the library that you have to meet. He's an anti-EMF activist. He doesn't use phones, but I'll go get you his email."

That night my friends and I go to Frankie D's bar and dance to Johnny Rawls, a blues musician who's kind of famous. The place is mostly filled with tourons, and they're too shy to start the dance party, so, as usual, my friends and I jump in the middle of the dance floor and dance like crazy until everyone joins in. Of course we don't wear any shoes, and the bartender keeps yelling at us to put them back on, until Johnny sings a song called "Barefoot-in'," and the bartender shakes her head and gives up.

Gary

When I email Gary, he agrees to meet up with me and talk about EMF's. Gary has a program called Smart Shelter in which he travels around the Moab- Colorado area, distributing literature on EMF issues, free of charge, and giving free natural building advice. He is one of the world experts on electrosensitivity, and years later I am still amazed by how lucky I was to have met him at exactly the perfect time in my life (But that is how networking works, when you don't have social media).

Gary can be described as a tall dark stranger: 6' 4", often wears black (does it help with EMF, I wondered?), and, I realized the more I got to know him, definitely quite strange (in the most awesome way). He has had an illustrious career history prior to becoming an EMF expert, with experience in physics, an FCC radio broadcast license, a stint with NASA (a heat of reentry study for the Mariner Space Module), a career as a natural building architect, a touring singer/ songwriter, and more…until electrosensitivity exiled him into the wild lands of Colorado and Utah, where he now travels seasonally to different remote electrosafe campsites, helping to educate a network of electrosensitives along the way.

We meet up under the hackberry tree outside the library and sit down in the grass. He hands me a stack of pamphlets and tells me to keep them.

"So, yeah, I've been feeling electricity for the past few

months now. I can't use a cell phone anymore. It's fucking up my social life. What I want to know is, has anyone ever cured it, and also, what materials can I use to shield from electricity?"

"Well," says Gary. "Here's the thing: electrosensitivity cannot and should not be cured. Another name for it is ASDC: advanced sensory discriminatory capability. It is a completely normal reaction of the most superior, functional and acutely sensitive metabolisms to anomalies in synthetic electromagnetic radiations. The fact that you're here at all and asking questions is proof that you're superior to the masses of humans who can't tell their ass from a hole in the ground." He gestures over to the Visitor Center across the street, where a herd of tourons is currently waddling across the parking lot, most of them with cell phones in hand.

"That makes sense," I said. "I always thought that people were stupid for not noticing this stuff. But what can I do about it in my life?"

"Avoidance is best," he says. "You see, the problem is not with you, it's with the environment...a condition known as full-function impairment...remove the electrosensitive from the fields, and the problem goes away. The key is locating the white zones- places free of synthetic radiation- and creating micro habitats powered by DC current and passive solar."

"I live without any electricity at all," I say. "But sometimes I worry about what the wireless radiation levels are where I live, at The Land." Gary knew about The Land, from Beana.

"If you want, I can come out there next weekend, and give you a consultation," he says. "I'll bring my meters and we can test what the radiation levels are, and we can take a look at your living situation."

"That would be awesome," I say.

"Meet me here about 1:00 on Saturday," Gary says. "Now if you'll excuse me, it's about time for this kid to be getting the fuck out of Dodge."

Shouldering the backpack filled with wild plants, fruit, and books, I walk down Moab's congested Main Street to Matrimony Spring, put my thumb out and make my way up to the cabin. I stay there for a few days, making fires in the wood stove and drinking herbal tea and reading Gary's stack of introductory pamphlets on surviving electrosensitivity (or ASDC, as he calls it). Becoming electrosensitive had been like having a first grade education and then getting thrown into college, with no allowance for the cafeteria and no dorm room, homeless and having to sneak into classes to somehow pass the tests…and now, having these pamphlets feels like I've finally been given the textbooks. It's like I'm a member of an exclusive, secret club- one that I would have preferred not to be a part of- but I'm here now, and I'll admit it, it's kind of exciting. And overwhelming.

Gary has a no-nonsense way of describing electromagnetic pollution that I appreciate. He says, in the pamphlet "Chivalry and the Wireless Age" (part of The ADSC Standard):

"We live in an extraordinary era in the development of

manmade capabilities for handling electromagnetic phenomenon. Electronic engineering's maturity, as it is found here at the early end of the New Millennium, is exactly equivalent in professional and competent scientific development to that of the sewage treatment systems in use in the urban ghettos of Medieval Europe, in which human waste was considered competently disposed of by collecting it in urns and pots which were emptied out the windows of domiciles onto the streets below...hence the convention of chivalrous decorum, which lasts all but to this day, in which men are instructed to walk on the outside of sidewalks wearing broad brimmed hats...protecting their clad damsels strolling inside closer to the building, away from the expected trajectories of the globs of fetid residue descending from the heavens and windows above."

And later in the pamphlet:

"The EHS community now mandates that there is no such thing as safe wireless communication...in any form...or in any way. We further mandate that all manmade synthetic electromagnetic radiation be contained within the components manufacturing it in a way so that zero...none...nada...as in not one fucking bit of it...is emitted or leaked beyond the physical boundaries of the device's enclosure and that all transmissions used for communication and power generation be contained within solid metallic conductors, properly shielded so as to emit zero detectable radiation, and that these conductors be buried in the ground with all the rest of our sewage disposal transmission and processing infrastructure with hardwired connectivity, not wireless routers.

This is not a request. It is a criterion for continued existence of those responsible."

The pamphlets go into EHS symptoms (of which I have many), the levels of sensitivity (I believe I'm an Alpha Two), corruption in the cell phone industry (it is rampant), and practical solutions to living in remote wild locations with a minimalist lifestyle. There are also the highly entertaining Mustang Ranch stories, which are about a fictional group of electrosensitives who live at a nudist hot springs community somewhere between Moab and Monticello. In one story, the characters go to Moab to bust up a bunch of Smart meters (with the help of their invisible Indian friend), and in another, their pet Pterodactyl (which Gary insists on calling a Teradactyl) shits all over a lady who has the audacity to make a cell phone call.

Gary has this complicated, hand-drawn chart, called the "Gary Chart," of the Electromagnetic Spectrum and all the different frequencies, including which frequencies are utilized by various electrical devices. I studied it in the morning with strong coffee, and eventually it all began to make sense.

Electricity and Life

This is the electromagnetic spectrum. It is organized here from low frequency to high frequency, and comprises all the frequencies of electricity we have so far been able to measure, with radio waves at the bottom and gamma rays at the top. All of these waves move at the speed of light.

The bottom part up to UV light is classified as non-ionizing, and the top part from extreme UV to gamma rays is classified as ionizing, which means that it knocks electron off atoms ("Conventional" science says that it is only the ionizing part of the spectrum that is harmful to biological life. "Conventional" science has also been shown to be full of shit on more than one occasion).

Frequency, measured in Hertz= cycles per second.
Megahertz=million hertz,
Gigahertz=billion hertz
Wavelength= how long the waves are, which is inversely proportional to the frequency
Amplitude= how high the waves are
Volt= how much pressure there is in an electrical circuit. The higher the voltage, the more electrical current.

ELECTROMAGNETIC SPECTRUM

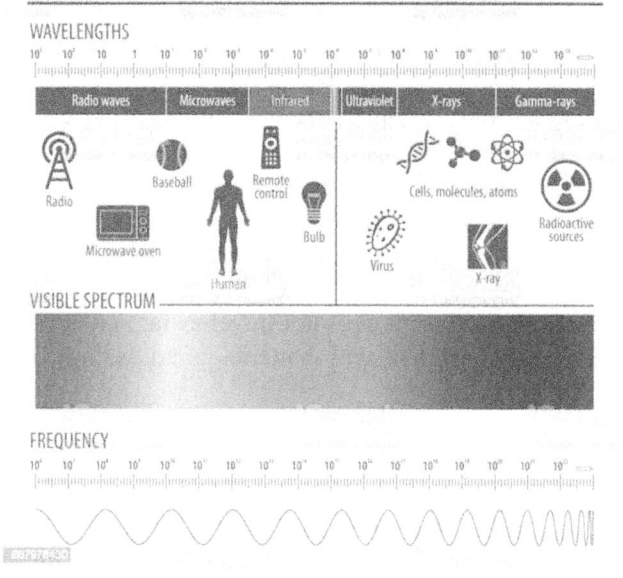

WAVELENGTHS

| Radio waves | Microwaves | Infrared | Ultraviolet | X-rays | Gamma-rays |

- Radio
- Baseball
- Microwave oven
- Human
- Remote control
- Bulb
- Cells, molecules, atoms
- Virus
- X-ray
- Radioactive sources

VISIBLE SPECTRUM

FREQUENCY

DC Electricity

DC stands for direct current and has waves that flow in one direction only. Straight and to the point. It flows from positive to negative.

Using DC power as an electrical source is generally considered harmless to biological life (an oversimplification, but it will do for our purposes here). You can put up a solar panel and have instant, safe power, but only when the sun is shining. Or, you can store it in batteries (which are the expensive part), and then have safe power whenever you want. DC can easily power lights, and it can power a fridge if you buy a DC fridge. It works well for trailers and tiny houses, but is not commonly used in large houses with a lot of appliances, because it does not travel as far and is not as efficient. A flashlight with batteries is an example of a DC field.

AC Electricity

AC stands for Alternating Current. It alternates between positive and negative polarity, changing direction lots of times. The amount of times it alternates per second, or cycles per second, is measured in Hertz (hurts). AC household power in America is 60 Hertz, in Europe it is 50 Hertz. These frequencies just happen to line up with the frequencies of extreme stress in humans. Coincidence?

All of the frequencies commonly encountered in modern life are alternating current: this includes radio waves,

Wi-Fi, and household power. Battery-operated devices that have a motor are putting out AC as well. AC is rare in nature, but it is found in lightning.

Magnetics

To complicate things, all electric waves give off a magnetic field. The field is at right angles to the direction of the wave.

If all this seems complicated, consider what a leading physicist once told Gary after he asked her, at the end of a long conference, "So what is magnetism, really?"

"Honestly?" She'd said. "We have no idea."

A Typical Day for a Desert Rat

"So do you live here in Moab?" My ride asks as I hop in the backseat of the rental minivan. I have my backpack, filled with apples from the tree behind Frankie D's, and I'm carrying a pumpkin (after Halloween I go "trick-or-treating" for pumpkins, which I cook). I'm hitchhiking to The Land (I could walk the nine miles and don't mind the walk, but I don't want to walk under those high-voltage lines. The car is quicker. Though I don't like the feel of these new electronic cars).

"Yup. Got stranded here three years ago, never left. Best mistake I ever made."

They laugh and the wife snaps a picture out the window of some petroglyphs. They're a nice family from Ohio or Massachusetts or New Jersey: tourists, or tourons as we affectionately call them here in Moab. Hundreds of rides over the years, faces blend together and blur into a conglomerate of all the people who pass through this place in space and time. They let me out when they reach their hiking spot, and I continue along the road to The Land.

Quieter out this far. Red cliffs tower above like high rise office buildings on Mars. Ravens croaking. Soft scuff scuff of dusty Crocs on dusty ground. This pumpkin is getting heavy. Open the cattle gate, walk though the cottonwoods, grab a few handfuls of wild mustard greens for dinner tonight as I go. Walk the last mile down our driveway to The Land.

And then, my comfortable space in the rocks. A rock ledge just high enough to sit up in bed (which is an old mattress on pallets), a fire pit to cook the pumpkin and greens while I read some new pamphlets from Gary (he left them for me in my "mailbox," a plastic case hidden under a pallet outside the coffeeshop in town). I can sit here in the quiet of evening and look out across the desert, and the stage (for music events), the old cars, the backhoe, the ten or so couches, assorted garbage strewed across the main area. A fluffy black and white cat, Cleo, purrs against my ankles.

Luckily, the party is not here tonight. A new crop of beer cans is evidence that they have been here, but I've specifically timed my stay to be on a weekend. Probably the partiers will just pass out after the bar, and hopefully none of them will be ambitious enough to drive out here with their booze and their noise and their cell phones. No guarantee though. I don't sleep that well here anymore, knowing that humans could show up anytime without warning. Need to find a new rock soon.

Actually my whole vibe with Moab is getting more and more negative these days, despite the happy persona I put on for the tourists. Moab itself is no longer the kind of place where you can walk barefoot down the middle of the street on a Sunday morning drinking coffee. Now, every week is Jeep Week, and the tourons and their machines fill the air with horrible sounds, cell phone signals, and the stench of ATV smoke and bug spray. And me: I'm nauseous, something in my guts is always swelling, like there's an alien in there wanting to pop out, and those spots on the right side of my head are constantly buzzing whenever I'm near anything electric.

The backpack feels heavier than it used to. My whole existence feels heavier, like I'm not doing this desert rat lifestyle for fun anymore.

What drives me nuts is that I need civilization. Tumbleweeds and the occasional rock squirrel aren't enough to sustain me. I need the health food store, and the Dumpster (Village Market's Dumpster often contains boxes of organic bananas and other fresh produce). To get to these, I need to walk or hitchhike every few days into Electromagnetic Hell. I'm extremely disorganized and have stashes of food and supplies under various rocks between here and Castle Valley. I can't fit it all in one backpack. It seems like I spend half my time just managing stuff. Why can't I just be simple like an animal? Why do humans need all this shit? And the addictions: half the time when I subject myself to Moabylon's rigors, it's not even a survival situation when I need groceries.

Sometimes I just want a chocolate bar. Or an iced coffee (with coffee ice cubes in it, and almond milk....mmmmm....). Or I just want to socialize. But everyone has a cell phone these days. It's like they're turning into cyborgs. What the fuck.

My shelter in the rocks

This is your Brain on Twitter

Years ago, my brother showed me a website where you could listen to audio files of sound frequencies designed to mimic the effects of different drugs. You clicked on the drug you wanted, put on headphones, and supposedly the frequency would cause your brainwaves to mimic the effects of the drug. The first listen for each drug was free, after that it cost a dollar.

I picked acid, put on my headphones and hit play. Some trippy sounds, and I really could feel my mind expanding, becoming suggestible...it really did feel like the early stages of just before the acid kicks in. Next, I picked the crystal meth file. I've never done meth, so I don't know for sure what it would feel like, but the digital, disjointed noise induced in me a dark, creepy, paranoid kind of sensation. I took the headphones off after less than a minute. Somehow I didn't want to listen to any more files.

If you take a sound file, increase the frequency out of the audio range but keep the same waveform, you can create biological, psychological effects (and you can do the reverse: take your Cornet meter or Acoustimeter, plug in the headphones, and listen to what a Wi-Fi signal sounds like. It's not pretty).

We are beings of frequency. These things affect us at a deep level. Cell phone and video game programmers know this, and knowingly program druglike frequencies into these devices. Same thing with Blu-ray televisions. Ever wonder why you go into a trance and can't look away?

Most humans are or have been addicted to something. It's the human condition on Earth right now. It can take years of deprogramming to get free of these things. And the thing you have to realize is, people will do anything to defend their addictions.

How many times has an addict told you, "Oh, just have a beer, just one won't hurt you." Or, "I don't have a coke problem, I just do a line or two at parties, I can quit anytime." Or, at the McDonald's drive-thru, "I'll eat healthy tomorrow. I'm just too busy to cook tonight." Why would wireless addiction be any different?

What if there was a drug which could do your online banking, order a pizza, check your blood pressure, check the stock market, research any subject in the world you wanted, play any song in the world you wanted, call Grandma, find you a date, and shop online for anything in the world you wanted at the click of a button? Can you think of any better dopamine release trigger? And then add on to that all the invisible, addictive frequencies...do you see how dangerous this would be?

What if the whole world was addicted to this thing, which was not only socially acceptable, but not using it makes you a pariah (way more uncool than turning down a cigarette from your school buddies back in the day), and you tried to tell the whole world that their drug was making you sick and it could make them sick too? Have you ever tried to get between an addict and their drugs? What do you think is going to happen?

That, my fellow electrosensitives, is why your friends and family can't believe you.

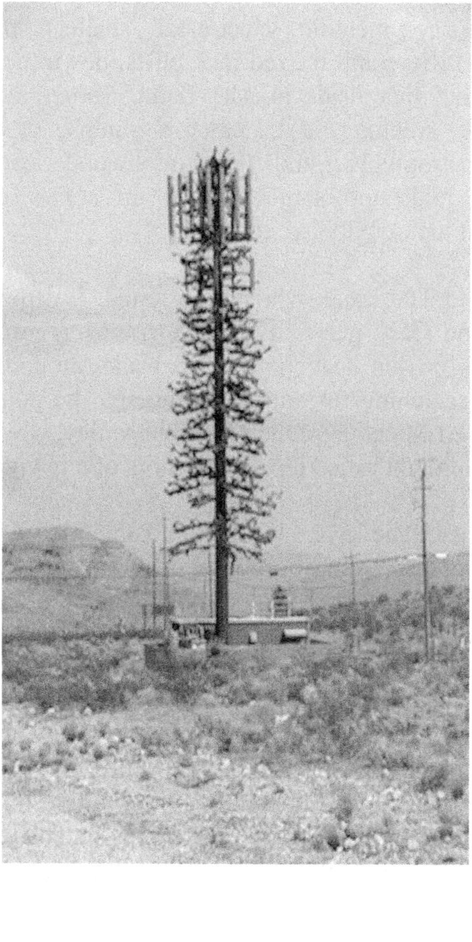

EMF School, Day One

I'm riding on the back of Gary's truck in a box he's building out of 2X4's (the first stage of what will be a portable, non-metallic, electrosafe shelter), past the Colorado River and the red rock cliffs, down the windy, dusty road that leads to The Land. Some ravens fly overhead, croaking, and I catch a glimpse of bighorn sheep petroglyphs, and the cottonwood leaves are turning gold, and some tourons on ATVs give us quizzical looks. I do love my life.

We get to The Land, which is deserted. I dismount the truck, and Gary gets out his Acoustimeter, turns it on and puts on his headphones. He walks around, like a dowser searching for buried springs, but he points it at the new BLM campground across the valley, where I can see the sunlight reflecting off the roofs of a few vehicles.

"Over there," he says. "I'm getting something. Probably a car booster from those motor maggots. Otherwise there's not much here, I'm not getting anything from the property."

He hands the meter to me, and I put on the headphones. There is indeed an annoying sound of Dark Force Energy coming from across the valley, like starlings chirping on a power line, but it is faint. Interestingly, the sound is strongest at the site of the new outhouse, where I have sometimes felt there was a signal. We walk over to my shelter.

"This is cool," says Gary, looking at my stone walls. "I

can see how it maximizes the solar exposure, and how this crack in the rocks funnels up the smoke from the fire pit."

"Yeah, I love it. I didn't know what I was doing, just picked up a rock one day and starting stacking them. It's too close to the party, though. I'll show you the new shelter I'm building."

We take a walk up the slickrock, past a rock art piece of a cat, and up a well-worn rock-lined path to my "Upper House," which is a bunch of boulders leaning against each other with a long stone wall surrounding the "yard." I have four metal barrels here filled with my stuff, a couch, and a shelf under the rocks filled with bottles of dried herbs and storable food. There is a space underneath one of the boulders just big enough to sleep under if it rains. The plan is to build a roof over the pile of boulders and somehow stack rocks to enclose it.

"It's a work in progress," I tell him. "Don't really know what I'm doing." Gary puts on the headphones and says the signal is even lower up here, especially when we sit down low behind the boulders.

"I knew it," I say. "I always liked to sit in this spot right here."

"The most accurate meter there is," says Gary, "Is the meter between your ears. Always pay attention to how you feel."

I get out my notebook now, because I have a hundred questions and I know our time is limited.

"How far do I have to be from an electrical field for it to be safe?" I ask.

"That depends," says Gary. "A wireless field extends theoretically forever.

I wouldn't want to be within a city block of a cell phone. For household AC power, generally four feet away is okay." He draws a graph in my notebook of a descending curve that bottoms out at four feet.

"You do need to be aware of the concept of 'dirty electricity.' That's when too many circuits disrupt the AC to control and send it to different places, and it gets dirtied up in the process of having electronic devices plugged in. So you go from having a nice smooth sine wave...-" He draws a curve- "Which is still harmful, but much more so when it gets like this from being disrupted." He draws a curve with a bunch of jagged scribble over it. "This contaminates all circuits in the house and changes it all to dirty electricity. So, no grid power is safe, and solar-powered houses with inverters are even worse."

"So how do we block it?"

"Biologically absorbent materials are the solution," says Gary. "Long chain hydrocarbons intercept and absorb parts of the EMF spectrum. The different materials absorb different parts of the spectrum, so using layers of different biological compounds is best...plywood, plastic, sand, styrofoam..."

"I'm going to use sandbags for this house," I say.

"That's great…sand, which is silica, only allows electrons to pass through in one direction, and if you have sandbags filled with thousands of grains of sand, the EMF can't find a straight line through. Though sandbags are piss-poor for insulation," he adds.

I scoop up a handful of sand and let it run through my fingers.

"Now remember," says Gary, "These materials will only block the electric component of an electromagnetic field. Almost nothing blocks a magnetic field."

"Can we make an opposing magnetic field?" "Could be dangerous."

"These are the spots on my head that hurt when I'm around EMFs," I tell Gary, pointing to them.

"That's interesting," he says, digging out a chart of acupuncture meridian points. "Those points are on the gallbladder meridian, it's sort of a gatekeeper between the inside and outside world. Learn the Chinese meridian points. It took me a year to do it, but now after an exposure I can just massage the meridians in reverse of where the pain is, and the inflammation will immediately subside."

"Cool," I say, overwhelmed.

"You see, the meridians- areas of higher conductivity under the skin, which can be measured using a voltmeter from the auto parts store-there are twelve of them, and they operate on the body's own DC electric current to control all body functions and psychology. The meridian system is our first line of defense against manmade EMF fields. When they get hijacked, inflammation lodges in meridian control points, which are the acupoints. Massage the meridians downstream first, and it will release the blockage. This stuff works."

I study the chart, which shows the meridians coiled in lines up and down the body, with hundreds of little control points.

"I've been trying to convince the other EMF researchers in the field of the importance of the meridian system, for years…" he sighs, "But many of them are stuck in their ways and still cling to the theory that it is the destruction of the myelin sheaths of the nervous system that is the cause of electrosensitivity."

He then goes into the politics of electrosensitivity, of the coverup by the telecom industry and his correspondence with the whistleblower Doctor George Carlough, who was an insider to the cell phone industry and later exposed them in the book *Cell Phones: The Invisible Hazards of the Wireless Age*.

"And you know," he says, "Some of the people who invented the cellphone are now electrosensitive and living in the forests of Sweden."

"Serves them right," I say. "At least they're rich." "No, they're like us," says Gary.
"Karma's a motherfucker," I say. "The whole thing's

really depressing and feels like a losing battle."

"Well," says Gary, as we pack up the pamphlets and begin the walk down the hill, "I didn't get into this battle to lose. I don't *ever* fucking lose."

The Alpha Levels

There are three (technically four) levels of sensitization in the progression of electrohypersensitivity, as described by Gary and based on hundreds of field studies. These are the Alpha Levels. Alpha means there is a reaction to electromagnetic fields. In the Beta system, people are not having direct reactions to the fields, but they are still getting sick (See *The Invisible Rainbow* by Arthur Firstenburg to learn more about electricity's role in cancer, diabetes, and other conditions of the modern age).

Gary says that it is debatable whether the Beta system even exists anymore and that with the rise of wireless technology the population may be thresholding into Alpha One (some consciously, most not). I do seem to meet them all the time now. And as I've said, I've noticed a growing acceptance of the existence of electrohypersensitivity in people. It's like they know, with some deep part of themselves that is untainted by peer pressure and corporate spin, that this is real. Then they pick up their cell phone and start texting and get all stressed.

Then they deny that they ever believed it is real.

Alpha One means you can feel electromagnetism, but you are not debilitated by it. These people may have "normal" lives, but if they use a cellphone for too long they start to get a headache. Or the computer. Or they may notice high-voltage lines and choose not to spend much time under them.

Headaches and migraines are a common symptom. Insomnia and mood disturbances are another. Others get tingling in the arms or fingertips. Other than these symptoms, the Alpha One is usually a person in very good physical health. People can go for years like this, and many never threshold any further. In my opinion Alpha One is actually the ideal physiology for a human. We are supposed to feel these things.

I was Alpha One for five years. The first thing I noticed was that my cell phone gave me a headache on the right side of my head when I used it for too long, and I also never felt right in cities. I felt this "energy" from cities, that I thought was the people, but it was actually the electromagnetic fields. But I could go into cities and stay there for awhile, that was the difference. I was just "intense" and "on edge" all the time, and felt the need to self-medicate with alcohol, tobacco, and lots of caffeine. I didn't sleep much, and I felt the need to go walking, constantly, for miles every day. If I had just followed my instincts and gotten away from the danger (which is technically impossible in this century), I would still be Alpha One and would never have become disabled.

Alpha Two means you can feel electromagnetic fields, and are disabled by them. We can still go to town, when we have to (groceries, mail, coffee, getting a tooth pulled), but it is extremely difficult and feels dangerous to stay there for too long. Symptoms may be deeper in the body, and more specific: I myself get nerve pain, twitchiness, and visual disturbances that make it dangerous to drive. I've also gotten these seizure-like attacks (no loss of consciousness). Vomiting is common for some people (I only have a couple times). Recovery may take a few days out in nature, or it may be instant…just how long it takes to feel "normal" after an exposure seems to depend on how healthy I am at the time and how much sleep I'm getting.

I believe that climbing the cell tower was what thresholded me into Alpha Two (this was after several months of stressing my body by partying, not sleeping enough, hitchhiking across the country, and sleeping under high-voltage lines). It was an immediate difference, and life has never been the same. But still, as long as I stay in remote areas away from artificial EMF, I feel fine.

The difference for me, between Alpha One and Alpha Two, was the loss of my ability to compromise (lie to myself) about electricity's affect on me: no longer was I able to just go into town with my friends and do "normal" things. Just walking across town, or through a house, became a strategic chess game where I was at all times aware of where the power lines are (walk on the other side of the street), where the towers are (take a detour), and which businesses have the worst Wi-Fi (don't shop there, or get a friend to do it). No longer did I have the option of hiding my electrosensitivity so people wouldn't think I was crazy. Now I had to ask people to please turn off their cellphone. If I visited someone at their home, they had to come outside to talk to me, no way was I going in there. I lost my social life and suffered crushing blows to my ego every day because of this. But whatever, it did eventually make me a stronger person. I guess.

Gary, myself, and most of the En Terra electrosensitives

fall into this category.

Alpha Three are electrosensitives who are so badly affected by electromagnetic fields that they have to live in specially shielded environments in order to be okay. Gary said he's only met about three confirmed cases in 800 plus case studies over the years. They feel magnetic fields of any device, airplanes flying in the sky, possibly the friction between water molecules in a moving stream. You don't want to be an Alpha Three.

Alpha Four is dead. You don't want to be that either.

Can the thresholds ever be reversed? Maybe, but it takes time: weeks, maybe months, of living in a field-free environment so the body can rebalance itself. Organic diet and medicinal mushroom powders, especially lion's mane, can accelerate the process. I believe that my experiences in Vermont (more on this later) did threshold me into Alpha Three, and that through years of careful avoidance, and lots of lion's mane, I was able to slowly move the dial back down into Alpha Two. "You were lucky," says Gary. "This is not easy to do."

Gary says he has seen only one or two cases of EHS completely reversing, and that is when it is caught early and the person is moved to a field- free environment for awhile and allowed to heal. Other cases have reduced in reactivity, after a period of healing. Also, he says that in many cases, after the twenty-year mark of electrosensitivity's onset, the person will often get a lot better and their reactions will reduce in severity, though they will still be electrosensitive. I'm over ten years in myself and am looking forward to testing this.

Rock carving of jaguar (made with hammer and railroad spike)

But I thought only Ionizing Radiation has Negative Biological Effects?

I can disprove this statement with an example that everyone will understand. Microwave ovens use frequencies around 2.45 GHz. This is well within the spectrum of non-ionizing radiation. But, you will notice, when you put that Hotpocket in the microwave, there are definite biological effects.

Sumi (Photo credit: Soula Marie)

Day to Day Variation in Sensitivity

Sensitivity within an individual will naturally vary depending on time of day, general health, amount of caffeine ingested, etc. I can handle a lot more electricity early in the day, when I'm in "go" mode. At night, when my body is in "rest" mode, any exposure can be devastating and will take much longer to remediate. It is very important to sleep in a field-free environment. On the ground is best (see chapter on Grounding). Caves are ideal. If you don't have a handy cave nearby, see the chapter on Electrosafe Building.

An interesting side note is that when I'm feeling sick or "off" in any way, my sensitivity to the fields is less, not more. This is consistent with The Invisible Rainbow's accounts of early experiments with electricity. In the late 1700's, when you could stand in line at carnivals to touch a Leyden jar and get an electric shock (people would do anything for entertainment back in those days), the experimenters noted that when people had a fever (such as from a flu), they would barely respond at all to electric shocks.

I had Candida fungal infection for twenty years, and I noticed that whenever I had a flareup, I was able to be around a lot more electricity without having a noticeable reaction. So I'd take advantage of those days to do my computer stuff, and to go to town to get groceries (not so good for the grocery list: the Candida said, buy ice cream, chocolate bars, salt and pepper potato chips). Could it be that Candida is actually the body's way of protecting itself against radiation? Not worth it, in my opinion.

I've also noticed a relationship between sugar consumption and sensitivity: if I eat a bunch of sugary crap, I barely feel the fields at all (but the next day is awful). Again, not worth it. The same is true of alcohol and drugs. I am sure that the modern epidemic of addiction (all kinds of addiction) is related to the rise in wireless technology.

Double-Blind-Studies---Versus. Observational Awareness

There are two ways of doing research on a subject like electrosensitivity.

One is the double-blind study method, currently the method that is considered valid by the scientific community. In this method, you first get funding either from the telecommunications communities themselves or from some government agency that is closely associated with them. Then you take a bunch of inbred rats, separate them into "experimental" and "control" groups, and subject them to torturous conditions that may or may not have any relation to the medical issue in humans you are trying to understand. After that, you manipulate the data in a way that your funding party agrees to, and then release the study in a prestigious medical journal.

The second way of doing research is what Gary calls the "En Terra," or "on the ground" method. This involves a lifetime of patient observation of yourself, other humans, and the natural world around you. You look, listen, smell, touch, taste, and take notes.

Take your EMF meter and start measuring the field levels everywhere you go. Measure your home, your workplace, the grocery store, your car, Wal-Mart, your favorite hiking spot, the coffee shop. Take measurements on different days and at different times of day, and see if there's any variation. How do you feel in a high-EMF environment? How do you feel in a low

EMF environment? Find a safe haven and use it as a reference point against which to compare all other sites.

Is there a difference in how you feel with the Wi-Fi router turned on or off? How do others behave? How do drugs such as caffeine affect how you feel? Are you affected differently at different times of day? How do you sleep with or without artificial EMF fields? Is there an increase or decrease in anxiety? How about appetite? Do you notice any effect on your pets? How about the wildlife?

This method of research can be influenced by your own emotions and personal biases, so it is important to be as clinical as possible in your observations, don't just "see what you want to see." There also are more variables than in the double-blind study (life is variable by nature). But if you keep observing, over a period of time, you will begin to see trends.

In conclusion, it is my belief that both the observation method and the double-blind study method are useful. The observation method is useful in the real world, and allows individuals to determine the amount of technology that is safe for them. The double-blind study method is useful for white lab coat scientists to further their careers, and for telecommunication companies to get the go-ahead to continue their agenda.

Double-Blind Proof

That said, you can do a search on PubMed and look through hundreds of double-blind studies linking artificial EMF to adverse health effects. Many of these are done by prominent institutions.

One major study was a 14-year long, $25 million study that was recently completed by the NIH's (National Institute of Health) National Toxicology Program. This study tested the effects of 900 MHz radiation (a frequency cell phones use) on rats, and the conclusion was that this frequency caused tumors, heart problems, and permanent DNA damage. Frank Clegg, the former president of Microsoft Canada, spoke out about this study in an interview. "Show me your evidence that radiation from 5G and cell phone towers is safe."

Another study, done by the Yale School of Medicine, put active cell phones above cages of pregnant mice, and cell phones that were turned off above other cage of pregnant mice. The researchers found that the offspring of the cell phone-exposed mice developed behavioral problems such as hyperactivity, which increased proportional to the duration of cell phone exposure, and that their memories were shorter than those of the mice in the control group.

The World Health Organization (WHO)'s International Agency for Research on Cancer classified non-ionizing radio frequency electromagnetic fields as a 2B Carcinogen (possibly carcinogenic to humans), in May of 2011. This was based on evidence that heavy cell

phone users have a greater risk of glioma (a malignant type of brain tumor). You can look it up on Wikipedia under "List of IARC Group 2B carcinogens." It is hidden in there near the end.
.

Electricity in the Medical Mainstream

You already know that the human body runs on electricity. What? Think about it. Here are the definitions of some commonly known medical procedures.

EEG is a test that detects abnormalities in brain waves, in the electrical activity of your brain. Electrodes consisting of small metal discs with thin wires are pasted onto your scalp. The electrodes detect electrical charges that result from the activity of brain cells.

Electrocardiogram (ECG or EKG) records the electrical signal from the heart to check for different heart conditions. Electrodes are placed on the chest to record the heart's electrical signals, which cause the heart to beat. The signals are shown as waves on an attached computer monitor or printer.

A cardiac pacemaker is a medical device that generates electrical impulses delivered by electrodes to cause the heart muscle chambers to contract and therefore pump blood. By doing so, this device replaces and/or regulates the function of the electrical conduction system of the heart.

Defibrillators are devices that send an electric pulse or shock to the heart to restore a normal heartbeat. Defibrillators are now kept in high schools, as high school kids now regularly experience heart attacks. Do you remember heart attack as being a concern when you were a teenager?

Electroconvulsive therapy (ECT) is a procedure, done under general anesthesia, in which small electric currents are passed through the brain.

So, these uses of electricity in the body have biological effects, and are approved by "official science" to have biological effects. Read between the lines of these definitions and you will see that "official science" admits that the body is an electrical system as well as a chemical one (the two actually work together). The reason why this truth is hidden between the lines is that to put emphasis on the body's electrical nature would mean that we'd have to redefine the way the body "officially" works, and therefore, re-evaluate the actual causes of health and disease. This would likely mean an upheaval of the entire medical system. And there are people in high places who don't want that.

For further proof that the body is an electrical system, let's hear it straight from the enemy's mouth. Elon Musk says, "We are a brain in a vat – the vat is our skull. All our senses and memories are electrical signals." Because of work that Elon and his minions are doing with Neuralink, the body's electrical nature is becoming more and more obvious to the public, which I guess is a risk the Dark Forces are willing to take while they prepare the public to accept their brain- control chips. We'll hear more from Elon later in this book.

Bliss Ninnies

The new EHS must be especially on guard for the unhelpful intervention of bliss ninnies. The bliss ninny can be recognized by his/her/their constant use of positive affirmations, an aversion to rational discussion of anything "negative," and the constant use of the phrase, "Tell yourself a different story." Often they are part of the New Age crowd, but not always. Bliss ninnies can come in many guises.

The important thing to remember, when confronted by a bliss ninny who waves his/her/their magic crystal in your face while lecturing about chakras and grounding cords (while ironically having no scientific understanding of the electrical nature of the human body), is that yes, what you are experiencing is real, and no, the bliss ninny is not a spiritually superior being just because his/her/their sensory discriminatory capabilities are not sophisticated enough to discern the fact that obsessively texting selfies of the hottest yoga poses to one's Instagram account in order to generate "likes," may be detrimental to one's health.

Gary and I have encountered quite a few bliss ninnies over the years. One of the most memorable was a woman who, in response to Gary's pleas to not put a relay antenna for Castle Valley's new cell tower on the roof of her home, replied that he should not worry, because she had checked in with her spirit guides on the astral plane, and they had said it would be okay. Gary, of course, said: Bull Shit.

Another bliss ninny experience was with a cranial sacral therapist (the healing arts are full of these people), who, while massaging my scalp, asked me for a description and history of my symptoms, so I described an experience that had led to a massive elevation of my electrosensitivity symptoms. I told Karen of the seizure-like event, caused by strong magnetic fields in a hospital in Rutland, Vermont, which consisted of a searing pain throughout my body that felt like I was being cut up by shards of glass. I was shaking uncontrollably, my vision was getting weird, kind of whiting out, and I had felt like something was breaking or being damaged in my nervous system. For months afterward, I had varicose veins in my arms and legs, my right eye twitched, and I wasn't able to get near anything electrical or even go in a house without getting a migraine. This description was given, not as a "poor me" type of whining to elicit the healer's pity, but as information so she could know what I was dealing with, and perhaps help me fix it (this was her job, wasn't it?).

But instead of saying anything useful, Karen told me, "It makes me cringe to hear you use that kind of language. What I'm hearing is that you think you are broken. I'd like you to tell yourself a different story, to tell yourself that you are whole and that you love yourself."

Would you accept this kind of diagnosis from a doctor or a dentist? I do love myself (probably too much, in fact). What I don't love is people taking my words and twisting them into manipulative psycho-babble meant to deflect attention from the fact that we are dealing with a very real problem here in the world (one that the bliss ninnies are feeding into, every time they check that Instagram account or download a new meditation app).

Listening to the bliss ninnies' advice can lead to problems with self esteem (Why can't I get over electrosensitivity with my mind? I must be weak; I must not love myself enough), and worse, can lead to you actually doing some dumb or dangerous things in the name of facing your fears (such as when I climbed the cell phone tower in Willow Basin). Don't waste energy on these people. Do take the part of their advice about being positive, it helps when you finally have to go to town and face the cell towers (because eventually you're going to run out of coffee). Don't wallow in self-pity, though, you're fighting an invisible war here, so buck up, kiddo, stop whining and be proactive, get off your butt and go do something useful. And do remember to take time each day for your positive visualizations, such as visualizing Elon Musk's Wi-Fi satellites blowing up and crashing into Mars.

Things Bliss Ninnies Say

"Tell yourself a different story."

"I just got a download."

"Stop being so negative."

"Just transmute the energy."

"I don't have the bandwidth for that."

"My spirit guides say…"

Bliss Ninny Paraphernalia
(some of this is helpful and not limited to bliss ninnies, so read on)

Magic Crystals:

I carry a quartz crystal in my pocket most of the time. They're pretty to look at and have piezoelectric properties that may indeed be slightly beneficial to the human energy field. I also put big pieces of smoky quartz and amethyst in my living area. I love crystals. But I still am electrosensitive.

Orgonite:

I originally said, "A conglomeration of crystals and pieces of copper, epoxied together. Bliss ninnies sometimes plant this at the base of cell towers, claiming it can "harmonize" the vibrations. Dynamite would work better."

To my surprise, Gary said he'd actually done some testing on orgonite and his meters showed there was an effect…though what, and how much it can help, is still unknown. Intrigued, I bought a piece and, I will admit, I thought I felt something from it (but it could have been placebo effect). I've seen YouTube vides that show the radiation levels on a meter go down in the presence of orgonite. When I did my own testing, I saw no effect. But, say orgonite's fans, it's the "scalar" waves that are being affected, not the electromagnetic. I'm not saying this isn't possible. I'm just saying it is not supported by the laws of conventional physics. Again, get some and do your own testing if you're interested. Put it around your living area: it can't hurt. Throw it at cell towers if you want. But please don't try to make it if you are chemical sensitive (and all electrosensitives are); resin fumes could be life threatening for a sensitive person, even with a respirator.

Shungite:

A black stone from Russia that is commonly carried in the pocket or made into jewelry. I've found that shungite most definitely helps me with my resistance to electromagnetic fields. It is not the magic cure-all that some people claim, but then again no single thing ever is. I wear bracelets and a hatband. I've also painted part of my camper's wall with shungite paint (mix some of the powder, available online, with wood glue/water mix, or non-toxic clay paint). Shungite is available online or in crystal shops and is not expensive.

Testing with my Cornet meter, in a high-EMF environment in Grand Junction, Colorado, indicated a one-third reduction of the EMF level an inch away from my shungite bracelet. Later tests, in low-EMF environments, have shown no measurable effect. More testing is needed.

My friend Soula painted the interior of a cabin with shungite/clay paint, and the bars on a cell phone inside were reduced from five bars to on bar (this was in addition to several layers of cardboard insulation added, which also blocks EMF).

Inventors and engineers: if anyone can invent shungite-embedded clothing (made with cotton, linen, or other natural material, not polyester), this may be extremely helpful to electrosensitives. The new EHS must be especially on guard for the unhelpful intervention of bliss ninnies. The bliss ninny can be recognized by his/her/their constant use of positive affirmations, an aversion to rational discussion of anything "negative," and the constant use of the phrase, "Tell yourself a different story." Often they are part of the New Age crowd, but not always. Bliss ninnies can come in many guises.

Gary and I have encountered quite a few bliss ninnies over the years. One of the most memorable was a woman who, in response to Gary's pleas to not put a relay antenna for Castle Valley's new cell tower on the roof of her home, replied that he should not worry, because she had checked in with her spirit guides on the astral plane, and they had said it would be okay. Gary, of course, said: Bull Shit.

Another bliss ninny experience was with a cranial sacral therapist (the healing arts are full of these people), who, while massaging my scalp, asked me for a description and history of my symptoms, so I described an experience that had led to a massive elevation of my electrosensitivity symptoms. I told Karen of the seizure-like event, caused by strong magnetic fields in a hospital in Rutland, Vermont, which consisted of a searing pain throughout my body that felt like I was being cut up by shards of glass. I was shaking uncontrollably, my vision was getting weird, kind of whiting out, and I had felt like something was breaking or being damaged in my nervous system. For months afterward, I had varicose veins in my arms and legs, my right eye twitched, and I wasn't able to get near anything electrical or even go in a house without getting a migraine. This description was given, not as a "poor me" type of whining to elicit the healer's pity, but as information so she could know what I was dealing

Protective Clothing:

Beanies, shirts, magic underwear that is supposed to protect the wearer from EMF. I bought into this one once. A hunter (who was most definitely not a bliss ninny) told me about some silver-mesh embedded long underwear and matching facial hood, socks, and gloves, that he claimed shielded his energy field and allowed him to move closer to deer. So I got a suit.

Consistent with other EHS's experiences with metal shielding, I did notice some protective effects the first two or three times I wore this (it is likely that the metal changed the frequency of the fields enough that it took my body time to adjust and react to the changed frequency). After that it did nothing but make me look vaguely like a terrorist. I did put this suit to good use one time in the psychologist's office when I was trying to get Disability for EHS. I figured that even if he didn't believe me, maybe he would at least think I was crazy and give me Disability for that. Didn't work. I can't even fake crazy if I try.

Gary's EHS case study evidence regarding silver threaded materials of this sort come from Zhena, a

severe electro sensitive in Pagosa Springs, Colorado who indicates she has to wear such suits to go into commercial establishments, and Geoff Simmons who operates a reputable EMF shielding supply website whose testing indicates that indeed the fabrics work in field reduction, but not completely, as Zhena agrees, and not sufficiently for an EHS to depend on for safety.
So, try it if you want. EMF protection is not one size fits all. Just don't spend all your money on it.

Stickers that you put on your cellphone:
Why are you still using a cell phone?

Pendants:

Some people report positive effects, some report negative effects, and some say nothing happened at all. Gary's friend Ruth, an electrosensitive, reported a worsening of effects from the Q-link pendant. I have never tried any of the commercially available pendants, but I experienced adverse effects from a copper-wrapped crystal necklace I own. All in all, pendants are probably not one of the most cost-effective gambles. I'd recommend starting with shungite instead, if you want to experiment with jewelry.

Gary says, when I ask him what he thinks about bliss ninnies:

"The American Educational System…understandably as complex and impossible as it has to be just by virtue of its size and age alone…has, however, yet to fail the American Public anywhere to the extent exampled by the absolute idiocy concerning even the most basic elements of legitimate science and critical thinking as in the contemporary mental derangement of the New Age. If I get into this discussion, none of us…you, Julia, or I, are likely to have sufficient lifespans remaining to see the end of what I have to say???

So should I, or just thankfully keep my mouth shut and go piss on another hot rock????"

Inconsistency of Belief

Ever notice how the same person will believe you one day, then not believe you the next day, about the reality of EHS? Notice how the level of belief has an inverse correlation with how "zapped" that person is (whether from stress, EMFs, or both)? This all makes sense when wireless device addiction is considered as just another form of drug addiction. The addict will defend their "drugs," and deny the reality that they are a problem, when they are under the influence of the "drugs." Get them away from the devices, in a quiet place in nature so their nervous systems can calm down, and they just may listen.

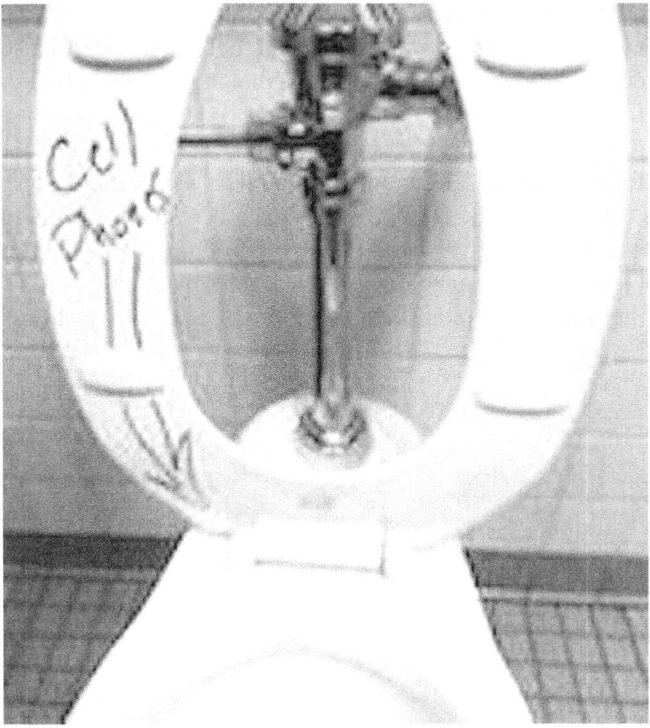
Cell Phone

How *not* to talk to people who don't understand

It is very important to maintain patience, a positive attitude, and above all to avoid victim mentality, when engaging with your friends who are baffled by your sudden onset of "psychosomatic craziness." I have certainly had a lot of people think I had lost my shit at various points along my journey, especially at the beginning when it was new and I was freaking out a lot more. How to explain to someone that what they do not feel at all, is causing me severe pain, and more importantly than the pain is causing damage to my nerves that lasts for hours or days after an exposure? How to make them care enough to turn it off?

Trying to survive EHS can create a constant source of tension with your non-EHS friends and family. New EHS is worse. Here is a typical episode from my early EHS career before I'd figured it out.

I'm outside reading under a juniper tree behind my friend Jarvis's house when I hear my friends inside having a discussion about whether or not I've lost it.

"Is she okay?" Says Jarvis.

"Yeah, what's her deal?" Says Morgan.

"She met this crazy guy at the library and he's convinced her that cell phones are going to kill her," says Troy.

I barge in the door at this point. I have to defend myself.

"You guys, I have really good hearing," I say. John Prine is playing on Kate's pink cellphone, on Airplane mode she says, but I'm having trouble concentrating with music playing and I feel spacey. I ask her to turn it off.

"I'm alright, you guys," I say. "I'm just having a low point this week. I think I'm dealing with Lyme disease again."

"There's nothing wrong with you," says Morgan. "It's all in your head."

"It's not actually," I say. "I get these severe nerve pains whenever I'm around EMF fields-"

"The pains are real," she says, "But they're from malnutrition. Which you don't need to have, just come to the bakery anytime and I'll give you some food."

"Thanks," I say, "But it would have GMO's, which my psychedelic experiences have told me are a cause of Lyme"

"Complete horseshit!" Says Troy. "Why is Moab overrun by fucking hippies!"

"I get this nerve pain that runs up my arms all the time and these points on my head hurt that correspond on acupuncture charts to the gallbladder and stomach meridians-"

"Acupuncture is complete horseshit and even if you do have pains it's because you're malnourished!" Says Troy.

"Lyme is a parasite," says Kate. "I've had parasites. It has nothing to do with GMO's."

"Electricity is the life force that runs everything," I say. "Artificial electricity fucks that up, and some people are more sensitive to it than others." I try to explain about the meridians in the body that run on electricity, but most of them are over it at that point, and I'm rambling and probably sound like a bliss ninny, so most of them go outside.

"You believe me, right, Jarvis?" I ask. We'd hitchhiked across America in 2012, and he'd seen the effects of cell towers on me, had felt them himself.

"Yes," he says. "But I don't know what the answers are, Julia."

"I'll have to figure it out myself," I tell him. We go outside, where everyone else is standing in a circle in the driveway. "We're good, right?" I say.

"Yeah," they all say.

"I can't be hatin' on you guys. Can't do it." "I know." "I'm just going through some hard times- sorry to be a downer- I'll get through it."

I have learned a few things about human communication

since this encounter. Although I maintained my friendship with everyone here, my unconvincing arguments did nothing to educate anyone of the reality of EHS. If anything, they felt sorry for me, and continued to turn their phones off when I was around, but they still thought it was all in my head.

Now, there is a right way and a wrong way to debate the existence of electrosensitivity. The wrong way, as exhibited here, is to convolute the argument by mixing in stuff about Lyme disease, GMO's, acupuncture points, etc. You've heard the acronym K.I.S.S. (keep it simple stupid)- use it. Also, never cite psychedelic experiences as scientific evidence. It was all I had, back in the Dark Ages, but it would have been more effective to talk about the animal cancer studies, the clotting of blood exposed to electromagnetic fields, the experiments in the 1800's with electric shocks and the huge differences in individuals in how much current it took to provoke a reaction, and the coverup by the telecommunications industry of the ill effects of EMF.

If I'd had a meter at the time, that would have been even better. I could have shown my friends what their cell phone radiation sounds like when converted to sound waves, and I could have measured the radiation levels in different areas and proved an exact correlation with the spots that, pre-meter, I had naturally known that I should avoid.

Become an expert on the subject, and people are more likely to believe you. Read up on the electromagnetic spectrum. Catch peoples' interest with studies of bioelectricity in birds and insects, or with the experiments of scientists such as Robert O. Becker, who regenerated amphibian limbs using small amounts of DC current. Keep it light, be entertaining, be positive. Remember, "You catch more flies with honey than with vinegar."

Also…not to put you under pressure or anything, but…you are a representative of the electrosensitive community, possibly the only one your friends and family have ever met. Set a good impression. Don't be malnourished, living out of a backpack and talking some crazy shit. Take a shower and leave your tinfoil hat at home. Be confident, but not dogmatic. Don't expect people to believe you all at once. Don't let your ego control you. Plant seeds. Remember this, about life: "It's all a fucking game, man" (Thanks, Jarvis).

And if they don't believe you, so what? Do you know you're not crazy? (If you're not sure, go into the desert and come back when you have an answer. Make sure to bring lots of food, coffee, and warm clothing because it might take a while).

Psychology of Electrosensitives

Speaking of crazy, Olle Johannson once did a study of mental health in electrosensitives, and he found that the only statistical psychological difference between electrosensitives and non-electrosensitive people was that the electrosensitives were more likely to put up with verbal abuse from people. Now, this most definitely does not describe Gary, but I could see how this "taking shit" mentality would eventually take hold if someone was an electrosensitive and forced to live in civilization among "normal" people who don't care. Eventually, you'd be so sick and messed up from the EMFs that you wouldn't have the energy to fight people who threatened your ego, and you'd just "take it." Add to that that 90% of us are women, and that we tend to be empathic and care about others, which can translate into not wanting to "make waves."

I believe that sinking into victim mentality may be even more dangerous than the EMFs themselves. The EMFs can kill or cause cancer, eventually...but victim mentality causes learned helplessness and depression, and can cause you to not make healthy lifestyle choices like going for a walk or eating organic ("You just need some McDonald's, that's why you're sensitive and we're not," or "What, you're too good for my cooking?"),

which will weaken you and over time make you more sensitive.

Studies have been done on rats where, in one group, the rats were given electroshocks randomly, and in the other group, the rats received just as many electroshocks, but they had some control over when the shocks would come (such as, they got a shock when they pulled a lever to get food). What the study found was that the rats who did not have control got depressed and gave up on life quicker, and the rats who had some control carried on.

I've definitely succumbed to victim mentality at times ("Why me? What the fuck?"), it is hard not to, but mostly I've had to think positive if I wanted to survive. Feeling depressed? Tough shit, you're out of water and it's a two mile walk to the spring.

That said: if you are electrosensitive, it is vital to pay attention to your mental health. The combination of the physical trauma, plus having to deny that you feel anything, plus your loved ones telling you that you don't feel anything, plus having no control over when the physical trauma happens, may create a disconnect in your mind that could almost be similar in nature to the disconnect experienced by survivors of sexual abuse. If you are a "stoic" type of individual who tends to not be in touch with their feelings (and most electrosensitives are this way), it may be all too convenient to just bury your emotions, where they will fester in your subconscious like a rotten, pus-filled tooth, making it difficult to have real emotions or form meaningful relationships.

Please make electrosensitive friends or start a support group. Paradoxically, you may be able to find help online, as there are message boards for electrosensitives and a couple Facebook groups (of course this is easier if you have hardwired Internet). Don't lose touch with your other friends, but don't expect them to understand, and don't expect a therapist to understand either (I'm sure there are exceptions). You may feel like you are alone...but there are more of us than you'd think. And, with the rise of 5G, you're getting more and more potential friends every day. There's always a silver lining (and as we've seen, silver linings may or may not be helpful).

If you can't find any supportive people, find some animal friends to go hiking with you. Also, listen to books on CD, or podcasts, whatever you're into, just make sure you get to hear some human voices on a regular basis. It does good things for the psychology, and may be more interesting than the voices in your head.

Diet and Electrosensitivity

Can changing my diet help with electrosensitivity? Maybe not directly, but it can do a lot toward improving our quality of life. Here are some diets and my opinion of them.

100% Organic

Definitely a must for EHS, as chemical and electrical sensitivity go hand in hand. You can't always escape the electrical part, but the chemical part is easier to control, by eating organic. I've found that eating organic has pretty much eliminated my A.D.H.D. symptoms and brain fog, even when in an electrical environment. I'm still just as sensitive, but I don't feel like shit all the time.

No matter how poor you are, if you're electrosensitive you have to eat organic. Glyphosate (Roundup) kills gut bacteria and paralyzes the digestive organs, and if you're already compromised in these areas, you may find yourself with a digestive system that barely works, sick to your stomach and unable to take a shit regularly. Don't worry about if your friends and family members have a "garbage gut" that can process anything: they're not you. If you're feeling electricity, you're susceptible to chemicals. No exceptions. Go organic. It's more work to eat organic, but not as much work as being sick all the time. You can do it on any budget. It just takes planning.

Go on food stamps if you have to. Like me, you're probably a willful person who would prefer not to be on government charity, but get over yourself. It doesn't matter. Living with electrosensitivity can turn into a fight for your life. Make it as easy on yourself as you can.

Gluten-free Diet

Definitely worth a try. Gluten intolerance can cause massive inflammation of all parts of the body. It can cause intestinal rashes that look like poison ivy and last for weeks. Brain fog, depression, extreme digestive pain, diarrhea…all this fun stuff is my reward if I give in and eat that slice of pizza. I also used to get eczema on my right hand that would last for weeks, just from tiny trace amounts of wheat from when somebody didn't clean the cutting board or if they used the same spoon to stir their stupid pasta and then dipped it into the pot of food they were cooking that was supposed to be gluten-free. Many of my bipolar symptoms went away when I went gluten-free in my early twenties (the rest when I got away from artificial light and EMFs and went 100% organic), and indeed, research shows that there may indeed be a link between gluten intolerance and mental illness, especially schizophrenia.

One time, after years of avoiding all gluten, I decided to test if I was still allergic, by eating some pretzel Ritz crackers. Big mistake. Let's just say there was a bucket involved. And I was barely able to make it from the bed to the bucket, all day long. I can't even *look* at a pretzel to this day.

Of course, it's not always this bad for people, but, like electrosensitivity, gluten intolerance is something that tends to get stronger over time. Avoidance is best.

Then again, I know electrosensitives who don't react at all to gluten. Gary tried it for a summer and said he didn't notice a difference. The only way you can tell is if you try. Give it up completely for a couple weeks (this includes bread, pasta, beer, and most processed foods…read every label, or better yet, cook from scratch). Then eat a bowl of pasta and see how you feel. If you have a headache, depression, severe digestive distress or explosive diarrhea, you may be gluten intolerant (or, you may be using a cell phone…make sure to eliminate the variables).

As for me, I would personally rather climb a 5G tower, and at the top, make out with a gross, smelly, pimply guy, on National news, while goats screamed at me from below…that's how I feel about eating gluten. I don't even allow it in my kitchen.

Ketogenic Diet

I first learned about this one from a guy I talked to who was staying in a nearby cave back in my Mill Creek days. He told me he had a severe form of epilepsy, and that by eating a high-fat, low-carb diet, he was able to keep it under control.

Intrigued, I later looked this up and found that indeed, the ketogenic diet had been used in the pre-medication era for treatment of epilepsy. Electrosensitivity, being a nerve-related condition, shares many similarities to epilepsy. Would eating a keto diet help me? I knew I couldn't do this while living out of a backpack (you need refrigeration for meat), but when I moved to my family's Vermont house in 2017, I decided to do some experimentation with ketosis.

Long story short, if you decide to try this: it didn't "cure" electrosensitivity. I did experience some increase in mental clarity, and a temporary respite from the *Candida* (a lot of things helped me temporarily with *Candida,* but only Candex cured it). But I also got gallstones, and the high meat and cooked oil diet was likely a contributing factor.

Vegan Diet

While veganism is preferable to the Standard American Diet of processed food-like substances (and almost all diets are), my thoughts are that animal fats have a protective effect against EMF and that avoiding animal products completely may be a risk factor for electrosensitivity. Protein is probably not as important as originally thought; we need all nine of the essential amino acids, but we don't need massive amounts of them, and too much protein puts stress on the cells and is hard on the liver. But fats are critical to the body's health, and animal fats in particular help to rebuild the myelin sheaths of the nerve cells (the myelin sheath is like the insulator around an electric wire, which protects the nerves from outside EMF).

That said, too much meat can be even worse for health, and factory-farmed meat is a horrible thing to support (this includes factory-farmed organic, where animals are fed organic feed but still kept in horrible confined conditions). If I didn't have goats and chickens, and didn't have access to farms where I could get humanely-raised meat, and couldn't hunt, I would go vegan…but luckily I don't have to do this.

If I was going to go vegan, I would look into mushrooms as a major dietary source. Mushrooms are not plants- they are more similar to animals in chemical makeup- and it may be that they could be used to healthfully replace animal products in the diet. Certainly it would be more humane than eating animals, because mushrooms are the sex organs of the mycelium- the network of underground fibers that make up the organism of the mushroom- and eating them doesn't kill the mycelium, in fact, by gathering mushrooms you can help to spread the spores.

I would also look into spirulina.

Another option that some "vegans" do is eat roadkill. Sounds gross until you try it, but think about it- roadkill's about as karma-free as you can get (as long as you're not so hungry that you're deliberately running over the animals yourself!).

No Nightshade Diet

Nightshades are plants in the Solanaceae family, which includes tomatoes, potatoes, peppers, eggplants, and cayenne (and also poisonous plants such as tobacco, datura, nightshade berries, and henbane). These plants produce solanine, which is detoxified by the liver of most people, but some peoples' livers can't process it and it builds up in the joints, causing inflammation and arthritis. Most sufferers have no idea of the connection, but giving up these plants has produced a complete remission of arthritis in some (not all) people.

The Dog Food and Cat Food Diet

Uh…don't do it. Let's just say I'm very good at coming up with creative solutions to unique problems, but not all of my solutions have been winners. It seemed brilliant when I came up with it: how to do a keto-type diet, cheaply, and while living in the desert without refrigeration. I was dealing at the time with Lyme disease (or thought I was; I may have had Lyme, or it may have just been electrosensitivity all along). I'd read that eating meat while avoiding carbs helped with Lyme, and that liver especially would help. So how about canned meat? But they don't make liver in a can (without a bunch of gluten and artificial flavorings, anyway)…..for humans.

So I found soon found myself sitting under my rock on The Land, eating Chicken Lickin' Dinner out of a dog food bowl, with sea salt. Here's the thing…I liked it. Dog food, cat food, they were both good, as long as they were gluten-free and had no potatoes either. Some of it was even organic.

Then I got into the kibble. I discovered it was good with spaghetti sauce. It also was good with almond milk and bananas. Like meat cereal. Why don't they make meat cereal? It was so *good.* I found myself pawning my extra stuff so I could buy a bag of dog food. I would often pick dog or cat food over regular food. Dogs would stare at me as I ate it, and I'd growl at them.

I obviously was dealing with major malnutrition issues, and the pet food was just a temporary fix. Even if organic, I think it was probably a low quality grade of meat, and it was more of an addiction than a solution, kind of like how some people get addicted to hot dogs or Spam (though probably it was higher quality than that). Anyway, I eventually broke the habit, and I haven't looked back. Though sometimes when I'm feeding the dogs at Soula's farm I get a little jealous....

My Current Diet that Works for Me

100% organic, gluten-free, with animal fats to help the nervous system.

My advice is to cook from scratch rather than relying on processed, high-carbohydrate, overpriced foods in the "gluten-free" section of the grocery store. What I do is buy 25 and 50 pound sacks of grain such as rice, millet, buckwheat, oatmeal, and quinoa. I eat lots of squash, sweet potatoes, and other starchy vegetables such as beets and turnips, purchased from local farmers if possible or grown in my garden. I forage for wild greens. I use olive oil, coconut oil, eggs, avocados, sardines, and of course lots of goat cheese, goat milk, and goat yogurt. I try to include fermented foods such as sauerkraut and miso, as they enhance the microbiome and help with radiation damage.

Since I personally tend toward laziness in the kitchen, the easiest thing for me is to just cook a big pot of grain, and another of veggies, and just eat those until they're gone (not quite as easy as cracking open a can of Chicken Lickin' dinner or Beef Feast...sigh).

I eat seasonal fruit off the trees, and melons, and banana yucca fruits, and occasional nuts. And the occasional dark chocolate bar (which does need to be refrigerated in the summer here, but don't worry, it's never gonna last that long).

I've found when I'm in an electrosafe environment, my body knows what foods it needs. When I'm in a high-EMF environment, I have no hunger at all, but when I get home I get all kinds of weird cravings, sometimes for days, as my body attempts to rebalance itself. Chaga tea helps with this. Green vegetables do too.

The hardest thing to figure out was how to plan my diet around not having a refrigerator, but on this meal plan it is doable (except for the dairy, which is tricky, but cheese and yogurt can keep longer than you'd think). Fruits and vegetables don't need refrigeration, and neither do eggs. Cans of sardines, tuna, or salmon are good meat options. Leftovers go outside in a cooler on the porch in the colder months. If you're not frying or cooking with fats and oils, the food won't go bad as quickly, cleanup will be easier, and your arteries will thank you. I would have spared myself hundreds of headaches, if I'd figured out how to kick my refrigerator dependence sooner.

A root cellar comes in handy. Also check out the building section for how to build a low-tech "third world magic fridge" that works by evaporative cooling. There are also now small refrigerators that run on DC with a solar panel, and the technology is getting more efficient all the time.

Fallback plan for when you're really, really poor: have a 25-pound bag of your favorite grain: (such as quinoa, rice, rolled oats, or millet), a bottle of olive oil, and a bag of spirulina, available on reserve for when you run out of money. This meal plan, while boring, can keep you going for weeks, especially if you supplement with wild-harvested greens.

Wireless Refugee

It's getting harder and harder to relate to people when there's this invisible force that affects only me, and I have to convince them to not zap me with this force with their cell phones while still smiling and trying to be a good friend to everyone and maintain a positive emotional state.

"Why do you need to be nice to people?" Says Gary.

"I don't know, I'm kind of a nice person."

"Nice is overrated," he growls. "Nice guys finish last."

I start spending more time in the caves up Mill Creek near Moab, but further than I used to go, up a hidden side canyon that takes me a couple days walk to get there if I go slow. If I hear tourons coming or smell their repulsive artificial fragrances, I move off into the bushes and wait until they pass me on the trail. I imagine the Dark Force energy from their cell phones bouncing around the canyon walls like the twittering calls of mechanical birds, and I growl to myself and hold my nose. One time I wasn't fast enough and one shoved his cell phone at me and asked if I could take a picture of the family. "No," I said, backing away, and they looked a little startled and then moved on…I felt bad and thought that I should have just explained the situation. But my people skills aren't the best lately.

Up the canyon I might go a few days without seeing anyone. I build small hobo fires to make wild basil tea and cook rice and beans, and spend hours looking up at the dappled sandstone of the cave's ceiling while the canyon wren trills its lonely song across this landscape of strange red rock formations and scattered bushes. This cave is small, more of a ledge really, barely tall enough to sit up and read (I'm reading the Lord of the Rings books currently, I can't concentrate on the biology books anymore). My neighbors are white-throated swifts, raccoons, and an owl. The shadows move across the canyon walls and eventually it's dark.

There is no time out here but Canyon Standard Time. There is no purpose for me but to get through another day. I'm hungry, I want fresh fruit, I want protein. Anything different than rice, millet, tumbleweeds, and beans. But I'm out of money, I pawned all my extra camping gear last month to buy dog food (which I've since quit…but I miss it).

Then, for a little while, I move under a different boulder near The Land, out of sight in the Chinle formation above the cottonwoods above Jack's driveway. It's near enough that I can walk over to The Land and see friends when I want to, but off the beaten path so no one will ever wander into my camp with a cell phone. I bring the kitten, Myrtle, with me (one of two we kept from a litter that was born out here this spring), and keep her on a leash near me while I work. I'm excavating under the boulder to make a little room. For now I sleep on a flat spot in the dirt above the boulder, but I want to sleep under rock because I know the EMF's are in the air and it is important to sleep protected.

I have a scrap piece of grate that I put over a few rocks

as a fire pit, for cooking rice and lentils with tumbleweeds. I have a little bottle of salt stashed behind it, and a luxury- a bottle of olive oil. Coffee with dried powdered goat milk- another luxury. One day I even drink half a pint bottle of whisky, but it doesn't make me feel good. Neither does the fine gray dust of the Chinle formation, which I've heard is radioactive. Radioactive dirt or radioactive cell phone hell: I pick the one that doesn't give me severe instant pain today. The future can take care of itself.

I cough in the mornings and the cat loses her voice. From then on her meow is just a raspy whisper (Years later, Myrtle still resides in the rocks above The Land, one of the toughest cats I've ever known. She still can't meow, and runs to me whispering loudly whenever she sees me).
One day, I'm sitting around the fire pit on The Land with my friends Kurt and Shawn, two fellow desert rats who spend some time out here. Kurt lives in a beautiful converted camper in various remote locations with his dogs. Shawn lives in the desert, backpacking with an adorable little white poodle, makes his own clothes out of Dumpstered materials, and does not have much use for humans and civilization. He's smoking a rollie cigarette. Kurt and I are drinking Yerba mate. I've got some purple Dumpster taters, not organic but hopefully not GMO, cooking in a pot with lambs quarter greens I foraged. Shawn's cooking some Dumpster meals mixed together in a pot, which he calls "slop." Myrtle's climbing around on the cliffs with the other cats.

"Everyone thinks I'm crazy, I should just leave," I grumble. Kurt's three- legged peagle (pit bull + beagle) dog, pokes her head out from under the blanket and I pet her.

"I think you should stay," says Kurt. He tells me about how there is actually evidence that GMO's cause autoimmune fibromyalgia by blocking the signal of the nerves.

"They just think I'm crazy. They say, nothing is wrong with you, it's all in your head."

Kurt says, "Remember on Sesame Street that song that goes, One of these things is not like the other?"

Shawn says, "Remember your body is not you. It's like a rental car."

"Yeah," I say, "One with a lot of electronics that fuck up."

"You don't need everyone to believe you," says Kurt. "You just need a more consistent routine, a spiritual practice of some kind, and stop drinking fucking wine with the bonobos (what he calls the partiers)."

"Good point," I say.

Eventually, I abandon the camp under the boulder when Shawn, who's a stonemason, points out that if I excavate under it any further it could collapse on me. I go back to Mill Creek for awhile. And back to The Land. And then to Castle Valley to pull tumbleweeds for money so I can buy food and coffee (but there's a Smart meter that gives me nerve pain and it takes me a couple days to recover from one day's work now, plus it takes a day to hitchhike there, and another day to hitchhike back). And the hidden spots along the bike path in town where I camp when I can't walk any further and I can't make it out before sundown. It feels like I'm going in circles, and there's always a fucking Satan Tree.

"Are you going to still be doing this when you're forty?" Says Jack as he drops me off at a campsite yet again. "What about when you're fifty?"

Eventually I give up and apply for food stamps. Accepting government charity is a blow to the ego for someone who prides herself on being a hunter- gatherer. But what's more important, your pride or your health, I ask myself. Do you want to survive this thing? Or do you just want to be another victim, another "crazy" person who slips through the cracks? At least I have one less problem now, and can eat all organic without it having to be all rice and beans. Having hamburger to go with my tumbleweeds, and chocolate bars whenever I want them, after years of food uncertainty, is awesome. Maybe I can get my life back on track. Maybe things can be okay still.

Gut Problems: Universal with EHS

Virtually all electrosensitives suffer from digestive problems that in some cases can cause more suffering than the EHS itself. These can include IBS, Crohn's disease, gluten intolerance, acid indigestion, and especially the yeast known as Candida albicans. Sometimes these symptoms will lessen when the electrosensitive person gets into a field-free environment, but often they do not, as these are signs of deep damage in the body and take time and good nutrition to heal. I think the root cause here is the health of the body's membranes: the intestinal membranes, the cell membranes, the blood-brain barrier, etc.

A membrane is what separates one part of the world from another part of the world. Ever heard that song that goes, "Insane in the membrane! Insane in the brain!" It's kind of like that. The world of our small intestine is supposed to be separate from the rest of our body, a world in its own, though it is semi- permeable so that certain molecules can be absorbed through. The world of our brain is supposed to be separated from the rest of our body by the blood-brain barrier. And each of our cells also is a world of its own, separated by the cell membrane, which is a phospholipid bilayer with pores and ducts and gatekeepers that allow specific things to go in and out. This is the ideal, anyway.

In a person with digestive issues, the membranes have been compromised. The walls are crumbling. Microbes have taken hold of the cracks in the foundation, like parasitic trees breaking apart an abandoned castle in the jungle. Big molecules such as gluten, which previously just went through the digestive tract, can now pass out through the tiny holes in the intestinal membrane and contaminate the bloodstream. So can pesticides, or even natural plant toxins that under normal circumstances would be neutralized during digestion (solanine from the nightshades, for example, or oxalic acid from spinach and beets).

So, all these proteins and metabolic by-products are getting through your gut membranes and into your cell membranes and past the blood-brain barrier, and cycling around in your body causing inflammation and weird rashes, and meanwhile a bunch of parasites are digging into the torn up mucous lining of your gut walls, and the parasites are pooping out waste that makes you feel sicker, and they're crowding out the "good" microbe species that normally poop out chemicals that you need for normal brain function (isn't biology wonderful?), and also the Candida, the fungus among us, morphs from its harmless one-celled form into a hydra of mycelium that further colonizes your digestive tract and hijacks your brain and says: FEED ME! And you have to obey, and give it sugar, and this is like pouring gasoline on an already inflamed situation.

To further complicate things, there is a definite link between pathogenic microbe species and harmful frequencies. Artificial EMF has been shown in studies to increase the growth of certain pathogens, especially Candida. According to Jerry Tennant, in his book *Healing is Voltage*, Candida is endemic to the human body and its job is to decompose the body after death, but when the body's natural voltage is low (such as from pharmaceuticals or artificial EMF), the fungus thinks you're dead and starts to take over.

It is possible to reverse all this. I fought with Candida for twenty years (trying special diets, fasting, oil of oregano, garlic, Pau d'Arco, etc.), none of which worked, and I finally cured it with an enzyme formula called Candex. The way Candex works is it contains hemicellulose, which dissolves fungal cell walls so they are not able to grow. Candida doesn't stand a chance against Candex. I still took it for a long time afterward as a preventative, but it is gone. Amazing.

Recently I started feeling a few symptoms (cravings, lethargy, ear itching) again, so I bought another bottle of Candex, and I felt better after only a couple doses. It probably would be best to take this every day as a preventative, as hemicellulose also helps with digestive health.

It also is essential to follow an organic and gluten-free diet, and to get the right kind of fats for repairing the cell membranes (animal fats, especially from fish, raw dairy, or eggs, are ideal). You also need to recolonize with the right type of microbes, which are best to get from fermented foods such as sauerkraut, miso, yogurt, etc. It is best to make these yourself so you're culturing microbes native to your own environment.

pure
ESSENCE
Candex™
SUPPORTS BALANCED YEAST LEVELS*
Encourages Healthy Intestinal Flora*
Fast, Safe, Gentle, Effective*
80 VEG-CAPS | 40 SERVINGS
ENZYME
SUPPLEMENT

Phase Shift

Fall of 2016, age 34: my last epic hitchhiking trip. I'm sick of Moab, with its Jeep-infested streets, hotels springing up like tumbleweeds, new cell towers and everyone thinking I'm crazy: Fuck It. I've spent the summer working and camping, getting healthy, and am doing a lot better with the EMFs. I can handle town okay lately, as long as I don't get too close to obvious wireless sources.

One fall morning on a whim, I decide to hitchhike to Vermont, where my family owns a house in a rural neighborhood of a small town. I can get my life on track: find some gardening work, check out the holistic dentist in Burlington and see about getting my mercury fillings out. Sleep in a bed instead of freeze all winter. Hot showers. Bond with my family.

So I stick out my thumb by Matrimony Spring on River Road (one last time), and make my way across Utah, Colorado, Kansas, sleeping in fields of sunflowers by the highway and eating raw carrots and beets, and organic dark chocolate bars, that I buy with my food stamps at supermarkets. In Kansas I flag down a trucker whose original route was going to take him all the way to New York, but ends up getting diverted (something about a meat load) to Oklahoma City, and I decide to go there because Jack and his festival crew are working at the Backwoods Music Festival and I'm thinking it might be fun to join them.

From there I hitch to Arkansas (I get a ride with a guy

who shares possum recipes, no joke), where my aunt and uncle live, and spend a week hiking, swimming in limestone creeks, hunting for quartz crystals and going to church.

They buy me a train ticket to Connecticut, where my parents live. A week there (I do amazingly well even though it is the midst of Wi-Fi hell), and then my parents drive me to Vermont. Quiet, slate and granite rocks, creeks in the backyard, scarlet-red sugar maples. It feels like coming home.

Lucky for me (if ignorance is bliss), I'm unaware of the shit storm looming ever closer in my direction.

Vermont

When hunting for chaga mushroom, you must look for white or yellow birch trees, especially those on steep slopes or near water. Only about one out of every 500 birch trees will have a chaga as a symbiont, so you will have to look carefully. It is more like hunting animals than gathering plants. The chaga mycelium is a black and brown growth that protrudes out the sides of the birch, looking more like a football-sized clump of charcoal than like a mushroom. You use a chisel or a hatchet to gather this.

Be aware, because if you gather too much chaga it can kill the tree. Only gather chaga if it seems like the tree can spare it, and don't take too much. I just as often don't take any, when I find a chaga. I "ask" it first if it is okay. It actually does give an answer. Drinking chaga tea enhances this intuition, and also helps with being able to find chaga.

Looking back, my whole saga in Vermont (which ends up lasting almost two years) is almost worth it, just for chaga. I always had a crockpot of chaga going, the whole time I was in Vermont, and I'm not sure I would have survived the experience without it. Chaga is the taste of that winter, and of the north woods. And the dreams…but more on that later.

The Vermont house. I love this house that my parents inherited from my grandparents, this big ski house at the base of Okemo Mountain. It has eleven bedrooms, three stories plus an attic, a basement with pool, hot tub and sauna, and black and white locally-mined marble in the kitchen, bathrooms, sunrooms, and pool room. This was the most awesome house to play hide and seek in as a kid.

Grandfather was a formidable character, who built the house himself and skied until age 92, lording over the family like Stalin ruling the peasants of Russia. He would lecture me about various subjects, such as how girls shouldn't hike in the woods alone, and how I needed to go skiing more, and how wolves would eat me. Grandmother was the nicest person I've ever met, who would drink chamomile tea with me and ask me about the birds I'd seen after I'd blown off skiing to go hiking in the woods alone. Both of their energies still fill the house (along with all their junk), and I sometimes imagine they are watching over events here still (one very benevolently, the other very judgmentally).

My brother Max, who lives here now, is a musician who makes his own instruments and sometimes goes on tour. We do well as roommates, because we're both weird hermits on completely different sleep schedules (I'm a morning person, he's a night owl), so we both have the house to ourselves for most of our waking hours. I'm doing okay with the electricity in the house, so far. There is a hardwired phone and Internet instead of Wi-Fi, and Max is pretty good about not making cell phone calls near me and keeping his phone on Airplane mode if I'm around.

The neighbors' houses are set far back from the house, and most of the houses here are abandoned anyway three seasons out of the year. The off- season is this magical time when I can wander along empty lanes and cut-desacs, past tidy steep-roofed houses, under the sugar maples and white pines and hemlocks, and everything smells fresh and woodsy. I can gather wild edible plants and mushrooms and barely see any people. I'm actually going for walks around town lately, and as long as I don't walk near the Smart meters and don't spend too long inside places with Wi-Fi, I feel okay.

Maybe I can actually reverse electrosensitivity, I think. Then I can write a book and help thousands of people with what I've learned.

Gary is not into this idea, when I email him some sample chapters. "Julia...the corporatocracy spends millions every year, under the table, leaking and lubricating New Age woo woo gadgets and propaganda spin to conclude that EHS is the result of a fixable deficiency. By doing this as a dodge, it heads off the real threat to their market...the realization that there is nothing wrong with the electrosensitive.

If you write a book delivering your complex explanation of EHS with genetic, disease, viral, metabolic dysfunction causality...you're doing exactly what Motorola and AT&T paid marketing to get you to do...shell game the public into Pavlovian cell phone dependency and Danglehood (A Dangle, in Gary terminology, is a human being attached to a cell phone).

Write a book on defiance, hope and proactive solutions. Make condescension and intolerance the only socially acceptable action toward the Dangle Morass. The wireless has to go... no matter the cost or barriers...and genital neutralization of the perpetrators delivers the best assurance of this horseshit not propagating into successive generations.

But remember...there isn't anything wrong with you. You are the canary. You are the harbinger. You are the revolutionary...don't piss all over the gift. Pick it up and start swinging. Freedom from our own victimization is where this has to start."

Good point, Gary. What would I actually solve by "curing" a few people of EHS? Until the Satan Trees come down, there is no solution. However...I'm an herbalist. I can no more not search for a cure than a mechanic can not try to fix his truck that's billowing black smoke from under the hood.

My mom gives me her old Kindle, and I've found I can handle going to the coffee shop once a week and downloading a bunch of podcasts. Ludlow is a one-stoplight town, with only a 3G tower (not right in town), and it's a pleasant walk down the hill to get here. I can drink a cup of coffee outside while I wait for the Kindle to do its thing. Here is the knowledge I've been thirsty for all these years. The coffee helps with the Wi-Fi pain.

Once at home, I listen to the podcasts and take pages of notes.

Epigenetics in particular fascinates me, which is the study of gene expression, how the body turns gene expression on and off depending on environmental factors. Could there be a gene for electrosensitivity? Turns out there is, actually several genes which are associated with it, genes which relate to liver detox function and inflammation pathways. I take notes on all these genes and pathways, and try to match herbs that will up regulate the expression of each pathway (turmeric and cat's claw for COX-2, for example).

I also research subjects like permaculture and mushroom cultivation, and make plans to turn our whole backyard into a food forest and mushroom farm. I buy gardening tools at yard sales, and start digging beds and improving the soil. It's hard work because the bracken ferns keep taking over. They own the whole yard as it is, and "weeding" the yard means going out and stomping down all the ferns, which can be three feet high.

In the woods there are mushrooms everywhere, so along with the chaga I also begin to teach myself about the edibles. Boletes, corals, lion's mane, oyster, maitake…why did I wait this long in my life to learn about the mushrooms?

Oyster mushroom (Photo credit: Soula Marie)

Chemical Sensitivity

It is impossible to write a book on electrosensitivity without also mentioning chemical sensitivity. The two go hand in hand, which makes sense if you understand that the body is an electrochemical system. You can't have one without the other. What I think is that the electrosensitive's stimulus threshold is set differently from that of "normal" people, so that we notice things outside the reach of other peoples' attention and perception, and we don't have "blinders" to tune these things out. Annoying songs playing in the background at the grocery store can drive me to madness, as can a beeping alarm clock across the house. I also have amazing hearing and night vision. I can pick out distant bird calls without being conscious I'm even doing so, and I often overhear conversations I'm not meant to hear.

But it's electrosensitive's sense of smell that really gets us in trouble. Most people have no idea of the stench that is emanating from them at all times. Shampoo, body wash, hairspray, hair gel, deodorant, body lotions, laundry detergent, perfumes, sunscreen…all of these are made of noxious, carcinogenic, hormone-disrupting chemicals that surround a person in a miasma of toxic fumes that the EHS can smell if one of these people gets anywhere near us (and not only do we smell it, but it actually makes us sick. Some of us vomit, pass out, or even stop breathing when we smell "normies").

If this isn't bad enough, "normal people" also pollute their environment with foul odors from spray and plug-in air fresheners and scented candles. These things have no purpose except to be awful, and it infuriates me that people buy them because they think they smell good. They only think this because their olfactory glands have been destroyed by a lifetime of constant exposure to these chemicals.

If I was dictator of the world...let's just say that possession of scented candles and similar paraphernalia would be a felony, and that manufacturers of these products would receive a punishment worse than death...they would be put in a cell fumigated with Glade plug-ins and Yankee candles until they, too, were chemical sensitive, so they would understand the torture they've inflicted on chemically sensitive people.

All of these repulsive products are completely unnecessary. Dr. Bronner's soap can fulfill most of your body care needs (they also make a cream rinse that works better for hair than their soap does), and it also works well as a laundry detergent (the eucalyptus can clean off residues of conventional laundry detergent off clothes, although this may take more than one washing) a dish soap, and to wash the floor, toilet, or countertops (dilute in water). Cove soap is another all-organic Castile soap that is like Dr. Bronner's, but gentler on skin and hair. Apple cider vinegar, in a spray bottle, is an all-purpose cleaning product and kills more germs that the leading toxic brands of crap. Coconut or sesame oil works as a body moisturizer, and there are natural sunscreens, bug sprays, and deodorants that work (and by the way, people who eat organically have less body odor).

If you follow this advice you can save a lot of money (and possibly even prevent yourself from getting sick).

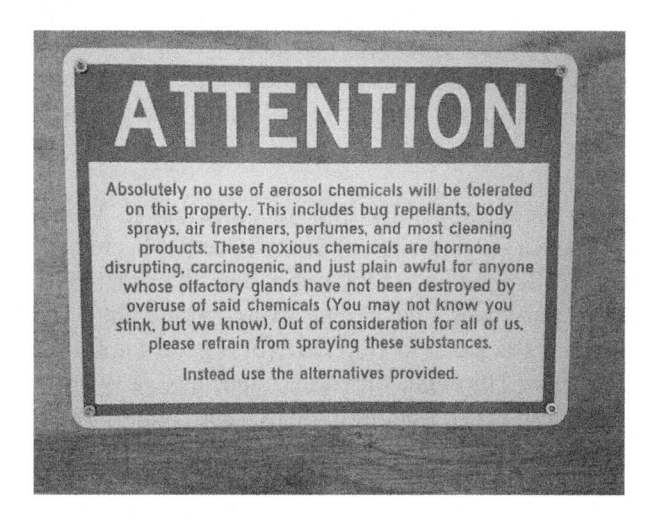

ATTENTION

Absolutely no use of aerosol chemicals will be tolerated on this property. This includes bug repellants, body sprays, air fresheners, perfumes, and most cleaning products. These noxious chemicals are hormone disrupting, carcinogenic, and just plain awful for anyone whose olfactory glands have not been destroyed by overuse of said chemicals (You may not know you stink, but we know). Out of consideration for all of us, please refrain from spraying these substances.

Instead use the alternatives provided.

The Yankee Candle Factory

Halfway between my parents' Connecticut house and the Vermont house, just off the highway in South Deerfield, Massachusetts and heralded by billboards screaming at you to come and experience the magic, is a terrible place that is like a cross between Santa's Land and Hell. The Yankee Candle Factory, spawning place of millions of miniature death-bombs such as Pumpkin Spice, Apple Pumpkin, and Pumpkin Banana Scone, has been churning out these monstrosities that are a plague on any person with a functioning sense of smell who gets within about a half mile of one.

On our weekend family trips to go skiing in Vermont when I was a kid, The Yankee Candle Factory was always a temptation for my mom, who likes that kind of thing. One winter's day, when I was about eight or nine, my parents decided to stop here for a good family time. We walked through the door, and into a world of Christmas trees, singing elves and candy canes, sparkling tinsel and of course candles, candles everywhere, all different colors and sizes, all just beckoning for me to come and smell them. I was more innocent then, and didn't know that something so evil could lurk behind the facade of Christmas trees and elves. I loved Christmas. I ran around the room, smelling each type of candle: Gingerbread, Balsam & Cedar, Christmas Cookie, Lemon Lavender.

Christmas carols played in the background as I smelled the candles: Rudolph the Red-nosed Reindeer, Frosty the Snowman, Dominic the Donkey (My mom recently told me about a fellow librarian she works with, who used to work at the Yankee Candle Factory and still gets flashbacks: once in awhile the library's silence will be broken by him going Hee-haw! Hee-haw!). I wandered through maze-like rooms of rotating trees, toy trains and elves, smelling more and more candles along the way.

Eventually we went to the cafeteria and I ordered an egg salad sandwich. Then we got in the car and finished the drive to Vermont. It was somewhere along the way or after we got there that the world began to spin. I felt the worst nausea ever and I lay on my bed and tried not to think about Ocean Hibiscus and Autumn Wreath and egg salad sandwiches. I don't remember if I threw up. The details are hazy. I felt horrible all day, and felt faint and woozy still the next morning.

I lost some of my innocence that day. And I was always a little more skeptical of any of my mom's bright ideas since then. And on every Vermont trip for years later, my mom would say, just to mess with me,

"Who wants to go to the Yankee Candle Factory?"
And we'll all (because my dad and brothers agreed with me) say, "No way!"

Doing my Best

Winters in Vermont last a long time. Although the sky is often blue, the snow is deep and the wind is cold. It's a long time for me to live inside. A long time in a house with AC power. With a microwave that sends surges of dirty electricity through the house's wiring, with a big screen TV, with people who always have a cell phone on, even if they do their best to keep it away from me. Although I don't allow use of chemical cleaning products in the house, they have been used for years, and that shit lingers. I suspect there may even be a Yankee candle or two hiding out somewhere. I should sniff it out and bring it to the dump.

I had been doing well with the electrosensitivity, but a long winter amongst all these trappings of "civilized" life is taking its toll. I haven't gained the weight back, and I'm slowly losing more. The scale said 109 the last I checked (normal weight for me is about 130). I make beef stew in the crockpot, and I'm always eating dark chocolate bars and whole cans of coconut cream, but I'm constantly sick to my stomach. Something hurts deep in my guts, all the time. Whether it's spleen or liver or a stomach ulcer, I have no idea, but it's seizing up after I eat much of anything, making me miserable and nauseous. It feels worse when I'm around electrical fields.

I don't like even having a light on in my room anymore, because it feels like it is buzzing. I also don't like my room. I know it is within range of the neighbor's Wi-Fi, because I feel it more by that window. I start sleeping on the floor in the upstairs marble sunroom. There are hardly any outlets in the sunroom, and it's in the middle of the house, as far as possible from the neighbors on either side.

I don't like being near the refrigerator. I listen for when it's stopped running before I go over to get something out of it ("Is your refrigerator running?" I think. "Not fucking funny," I answer). Then, when that becomes too much, I start just keeping a bag of groceries in the snowbank, outside the pool room door. I keep fruits and vegetables in the root cellar room. When I cook, I use the burner on the other side of the kitchen island farthest from the fridge, and I step back as much as possible. Later, when this becomes intolerable, I use a portable camp stove instead.

There also are certain other rooms where I don't want to be anymore. Most of them, actually. The kitchen and TV room are the worst, but the dining room next to the kitchen also feels intolerable (I'm not sure why). The main living room is one of the better areas, except for over by the computer (even though it is a landline, I still can't stand it). The pool room feels low-EMF, since there are few outlets and it is halfway underground, but the chlorine smell is intolerable (How anyone can stand this on their skin is beyond me). The bathrooms, which are marble-walled, are low-EMF, especially the one in the basement, so that is the one I've been using. Basically the whole basement is safe, except for the "electrical control room" off the side of the workshop. The middle rooms of the house, furthest from the neighbors on either side, are safer than the rooms closer to the neighbors.

Sitting in in the downstairs sunroom, trying out various herbs to stop the ever-present headaches, I can't help but wish I was more like my family members and the B&B guests, who can stomp around wherever they want in the house and eat sausage pizza with no thought about EMFs and stomachaches, who don't notice the stench of dishwashing detergent from halfway across the house and can swim in the pool and not notice the chlorine smell, can go skiing on the mountain and get through the Wi-Fi at the lifts without getting dizzy and sick…why is it only me who feels these things? How is this fair? What the fuck is wrong with this idiotic species? Where can I go to get away from it?

My dad comes up with the idea of hiring a builder to build a garden shed for me to live in. It will be like a tiny house, built with locally milled pine, with just enough space for one person to live comfortably. I pick out a pattern I like, and find the perfect spot, in a far corner of the yard near towering hemlock trees and the blueberry bushes I planted. (I use the Kindle with the Wi-Fi turned on to make sure it's the spot with the lowest signal). When the snow melts, the builder comes out and has the shed up within a couple days.

I sleep great in the cabin, and I love waking up in the yard to the sound of the robins and chickadees. I drink chaga coffee in a chair overlooking the woods, and hike in the National Forest and search for mushrooms. I hike all over Okemo and the surrounding woods, walking for miles along the railroad tracks, exploring swamps and stone walls and white pine groves. I do love it here, especially now that ski season is over and the mountain is mine once again. I savor every sunbeam, try to drink in every moment here in beautiful nature. One day I even waste twenty bucks on an alpine slide called the Timber Rattler, just because I can. I get in the little car and zoom down the ski slope, feeling the wind in my hair and a sense of freedom, like being a kid again. Then I continue my hike along the railroad tracks.

The days feel like a sort of timeless limbo, an in-between place in my life that is just on the verge of something happening, a change, just what I do not know, but this whole year has had this quality...I'm 34 almost 35, close to the end of a seven-year cycle and the beginning of another...maybe I'm just feeling nostalgic, looking back...but the days seem to take on the quality of a grace period, a vibrant fresh green time in which all I really have to do is live.

Herbalism for EHS

Connection to nature is what has kept me sane through this whole thing, and foraging my own herbs is one of my favorite ways to connect with nature. My knowledge of herbalism has made a noticeable difference in my pain levels, mental cognition, and other effects of EHS, and I can't imagine life without it. Also, doing something proactive, even something as simple as making a pot of herbal tea, is a way to participate in life, to snap out of victim consciousness and do something, even though there's so much in life that is not within our control.

Being an herbalist is like being an artist, or a cook: you can go through seven lifetimes, and still not be a master, and there are as many styles of herbalism as there are of painting or cooking. Here are a few of my favorite herbal remedies. I recommend you try them, or learn some of the plants in your own region that attract you (and there is something to be said for using local plants- often the medicine you most need is the one that's growing right outside your door). For herbs that don't grow in your region, you can get them in the bulk section of your health food store, or order online.

If you are foraging for plants yourself, always consult a field guide or better yet, get an expert's advice. There aren't a lot of poisonous plants, but there are a few bad ones that can kill you, and some of these look similar to the untrained eye to the medicinal ones. But it's not really that complicated, once you learn how to look: you can tell broccoli from cauliflower, can't you? Wild plant identification isn't much different. It's just learning to see beyond the "wall of green" and see the plant allies as something familiar. Again, this really has saved my sanity, being able to go outside and forage something that will make me feel better. On a related note, foraging for edible food plants is a wonderful skill for someone who is trying to avoid going to town, and helps to stretch the budget.

I have probably over fifty plant books, collected over the years. A good field guide such as Peterson's is a good starting point. Also, if you have landline Internet, YouTube videos are a great way to learn the plants and their uses. You can watch a video of an expert talking about a plant in its native habitat. But you can learn it all from books just as well.

I recommend using most of these plants as teas, because herbs in capsules are basically useless (you need to use your senses and taste the plant). Bring water to a boil, turn the water off, then add some of the dried plant, steep for about ten minutes or more, then strain through a strainer. I recommend trying the herbs on their own first, so you can be familiar with their tastes and effects before you start making mixes with them.

Some herbs are better used as tinctures, which you can buy, or, make yourself by filling a jar with plant material, then pouring in enough organic alcohol such as vodka to cover the plant, wait six weeks, strain and bottle. Use one to two droppers full at a time, and it's best to squirt it into hot tea as this evaporates off some of the alcohol.

I've put stars* on the herbs that I think are the most

essential for EHS. I like trying everything (my bedroom in Vermont was an herbal laboratory), but the conclusions I've come to is you should use local, abundant plants that you can grow or wildcraft, whenever possible. They are free and may be more effective.

Yarrow*

Yarrow is one of the favorite plants for environmental sensitivities. It is a beautiful, lacy white flower with green "chipmunk tail" leaves, and has folklore associations as a warrior's plant. Legend has it that the Greek hero Achilles used this plant to staunch the bleeding of his men's wound's on the battlefield, and the name, Achillea millefollium, means "thousand-leaved plant of Achilles."
Electrosensitives, for whom every day is a battle, may benefit from developing a relationship with this plant. It increases blood flow internally, or can staunch it externally; basically, yarrow "tells the blood what to do," which is useful since wireless radiation causes clumping of red blood cells. I like it as a tea (it is mildly bitter), and when I drink it I feel energized and alert, but not in a stimulant kind of way. If I had to quit caffeine for some reason, this would be my first pick of herbal teas to replace it. It goes well in blends with other herbs. I like it with peppermint and Grindelia.

Dandelion

Great for detoxing the liver and kidneys. Eat any part of the plant or use as tea. Make sure you only gather this and other herbs from places that haven't been sprayed. And don't drink it right before bed, as the French name "Pis-en-lit," referring to dandelion's use as a diuretic, means "Piss-the-bed" (not that you're likely to do this, but you might have to wake up a lot).

Red Clover*

Helps keep the blood from clumping, so useful to drink when exposed to 5G and other radiation. Use as tea.

Saint John's Wort

Use as tea or tincture. Elevates mood and is great for nerve pain from EMF. There are some contraindications here. SJW increases photosensitivity: don't use before a day at the beach, and some fair-skinned people may do best to avoid it altogether. And, as an MAOI, it tends to boost the effects of other herbs you're taking it with (as I learned when I got overly euphoric and giddy from mixing it with cacao beans). Also never mix with kava kava (it made my heart race), or with alcohol or medications.

Eyebright

Use as tincture. Amazing antihistamine herb for pollen allergy and skin hives. Also seems to have some promise as an anti-inflammatory after EMF exposure.

Calendula

One of the best herbs I have found for toothache (which

plagues most EHS from time to time, due to our hatred of the dentist's office). Use it as a tea. It takes down swelling of the gums and reverses abscesses. Also helps with toning the intestinal membranes. Easy to grow in the garden.

Prickly Lettuce*

The other essential herb for toothache. This common scraggly weed of parking lots and waste places has been mostly overlooked by herbalists. One night in the middle of winter I was screaming into my pillow with an awful toothache and I went to Soula's house and asked if she had anything for the pain. She took me out to her frozen, snow-covered garden and we harvested some dried leaves of prickly lettuce. I chewed these, and the pain went away. And I was able to sleep.

The white milky sap from the fresh plant is best, dripped right onto the infected tooth. The leaves also are good as a tea for nerve pain after Wi-Fi exposure; they help actually heal the damage. It will probably make you fall asleep, so only drink it when you want to sleep.

Chanca Piedra

The name in Spanish means "stone breaker," and has been used in South American folk medicine for breaking up kidney stones and gallstones. How it works is it dissolves excess calcium deposits, so it also works at breaking up the deposits in calcified joints that cause arthritis. Wireless radiation exposure is known to dislodge calcium ions from the cell membrane, causing there to be too much free calcium in the blood, which later is deposited in the wrong places, such as in joints or on artery walls. Chanca piedra helps break this up and flush it out if you take it before or after wireless exposure. Also clears out excess sugar from the blood when you've overdone it after a town trip. I believe it also alkalizes the body. It is best used as a tea (1-3 cups daily), and can be ordered in bulk online. It is mild tasting and mixes well with other herbs. I'm looking into growing this in my garden.

Ginkgo

Anti-inflammatory for the brain, and helps with mental focus. I sometimes add a little of the leaf to coffee or tea blends.

Rhodiola

An adaptogen. Pleasant, roselike flavor makes a good base for coffee.

Eleuthero (Siberian Ginseng)

Adaptogen that helps with oxygen uptake.

Lyme Disease Herbs: Japanese Knotweed and Cat's Claw

I have found a major overlap between Lyme disease and electrosensitivity, and that the herbs used to treat Lyme disease also help me with electrosensitivity, as many of the symptoms are the same. The two main herbs I have used for this are Japanese Knotweed and Cat's Claw. I have used these as a tincture (in the form of the LB Core Protocol, made by Green Dragon Botanicals, which also contains a few other herbs), and I have also used cat's claw herb as a tea. I have found the tincture to be extremely effective, but usually cost prohibitive to use just for EHS. It is the first thing I recommend someone do if they have Lyme disease, and I have seen it cure early stage Lyme.

For EHS, the knotweed and cat's claw are very brain-protective and strongly anti-inflammatory and help heal damage caused by EMF. Cat's claw is also an MAOI, and as a bonus it can give you some crazy dreams, similar to chaga.

Caffeine

I'm definitely addicted, and I plan to continue my addiction because I don't think I would have survived EHS as long as I have without this magic substance. Caffeine is a stimulant (obviously), and so is electricity. Since "you can't get more than one zap," I find that if I drink coffee before exposure to electromagnetic fields, my sensitivity reaction is much more tolerable. I think what it's doing is that it's holding the calcium channels in the nerve cell open longer than usual, so the nerves can keep firing longer (and electricity forces them to fire, whether you want them to or not).

Long-term, overuse of caffeine causes adrenal burnout and fatigue. Short- term, I need to get through today, in a world that's far removed from anything holistic. The plan is to live long enough to witness a world where cell towers get cut down and sold for scrap metal. So I'm going to drink my coffee.

I do limit caffeine use to morning hours only, and I drink Yerba mate on most days and try to save the coffee for town trips or when I want to get a lot of work done. I also highly recommend never doing any stimulant that is stronger than coffee, as stimulant drug use is most likely a risk factor for developing electrosensitivity. What got me the worst was those high-powered energy drinks. I was obsessed with them, drinking two or three a day at times, and especially enjoyed mixing them with vodka (Party like a Rockstar!). Terrible idea.

One good side to coffee, tea and Yerba mate are that they make excellent delivery mechanisms for other herbs, especially brain and circulatory herbs, such as medicinal mushroom powders, turmeric, peppermint, etc. I add these to my coffee/tea/mate for that extra boost. I also add raw honey and/or goat's milk, and sometimes raw cacao powder. It's the shit, man (Party like an educated, hard- working person who gets a lot done)!

Medicinal Mushrooms*

Medicinal mushroom powders are my number one most important daily tonic for living with electrosensitivity. They all enhance the immune system and the body's overall vitality, minimizing the time it takes to bounce back from EMF attack. I've found it helps to mix as many different kinds together as I can afford (I keep a jar of this in the cupboard), and to mix a spoonful with coffee or tea at least once a day (usually more often). I also mix the good-tasting ones like shiitake and lion's mane with food. The gross ones, like cordyceps, I try to cover up with other herbs or with honey.

Mushrooms are high in B vitamins and zinc and can help reverse the malnutrition caused by EHS. You can get the same benefits by eating mushrooms. I put dried foraged mushrooms into whatever I cook, which gives a unique flavor and tricks people into thinking I know how to cook.

The powders are best for daily use and most economical, but for acute situations mushroom tinctures are best. Here are some of the most popular medicinal mushrooms, but there are many more. I've starred all of them, but start with the ones you're most drawn to. The mushrooms will let you know.

Chaga*

Source of melanin, zinc, magnesium, super oxide dismutase, and just about every mineral the body needs. Extremely alkalizing. Great to take in a thermos to town and can "neutralize" the zapped feeling. Great as a base for coffee as it is similar tasting. May give crazy dreams. Don't drink at night if it's keeping you from getting good sleep.

I prefer chaga on its own than in a mix, and some forms need to be simmered for a while as they don't dissolve easily. I also don't drink it everyday, just in phases and more often in winter, but that is my personal preference. It also is important to not over harvest this mushroom, and I don't think it should be mass marketed on the level it is. Chaga is rare, it cannot be cultivated, and it can take thirty years for it to grow to full size. I sometimes saw spots on birches in Vermont where unethical chaga hunters had over harvested. Chaga should not be taken by everyone as a cure-all. There are many common herbs such as dandelion that will serve most peoples' purpose just as well for detox, and reishi is an easily-cultivated immune tonic substitute that does many of the same things as chaga. Chaga should be used by electrosensitive and chemical sensitive people, as some of its condition-specific effects are not easily substituted.

Lion's Mane*

Essential for electrosensitives. Contains nerve-growth factor to help the brain regenerate after electrical trauma. My brain definitely works better since I discovered this. I can have all-day focus as if I'm drinking coffee all day. The tincture helps after a bad Wi-Fi exposure; take some after town trips. For daily use, the powder is better (actually, I've heard the five day on, two day off schedule is most effective for neuron repair). Unlike chaga, lion's mane is easy to grow. I've wild harvested it in Vermont and cooked it, which gives the same benefits.

Cordyceps*

Also known as the creepy caterpillar mushroom. Cordyceps parasitizes insects and hijacks their brains so they'll crawl to a high place and die, at which point a mushroom spurts out of their heads and spreads spores. Luckily, it doesn't do this to people, in fact it's a great immune and longevity tonic for us. Yak herders in Tibet discovered it when they noticed their yaks eating it during mating season, and now it is popular in that part of the world as an aphrodisiac. Cordyceps is amazing for increasing oxygen to the brain, which is important when you're being 5G'd. Also great for adjusting to high altitude. Only drink in morning hours.

Reishi*

Immune and longevity tonic, enhances intuition, meditation aid, overall tonic for brain and lungs. Enhances sense of well-being. There's pretty much nothing it isn't good for. Known as the "Chinese mushroom of Immortality." I've heard chaga called the "king of mushrooms" and reishi the "queen of mushrooms" (Amanita muscaria is the court jester).

Maitake*

Balances blood sugar, good for diabetics. As wireless radiation plays havoc with blood sugar and can lead to diabetes, this is a great one to add. Also delicious tasting. I found one while hiking once and it was turkey-sized. I made a huge pot of chowder with it and bluefish, and felt great that week.

Turkeytail*

A medicine is made with this in Japan to treat cancer. In

America, the drug companies can't patent it, so they'd rather you not know about it. Nevertheless, many people have had success with it, including mushroom expert Paul Stamets, who cured his mother's breast cancer with it. Turkeytail is a polypore that grows on dead logs in the woods and breaks them down. I think it has a similar effect in the body and may break up cellular debris.

Shittake*

Delicious and also medicinal. Another forest decomposer that is detoxifying for the body. Great for the immune system. If you add this to your mushroom mix it will flavor it nicely and cover up the taste of the cordyceps.

Raw Honey

On Soula's farm I learned beekeeping and was able to harvest and process my own honey. I highly recommend beekeeping for electrosensitives, because bees are in just as much trouble as we are, and for the same reasons. If you've got an electrosafe place to live, you should definitely share it with some bees. They are very "in tune" with how people are feeling, and are more likely to sting if you are in a bad mood or not paying attention. Bee sting therapy can help with arthritic pain, and they tend to sting you on parts of the body where you need it (and there may actually be some scientific basis for this, as we know that surface voltage drops in sick areas of the body, and bees, which have antennas, use electromagnetism as their main navigational sense).

Honey is enhancing to the immune system, helps your body adapt to the local environment, and is soothing to burns, including the type of burning sensation we get from 5G and other cell towers.

Diatomaceous Earth*

D.E. is a fine white powder made from the fossilized skeletons of tiny sea creatures called diatoms. I give it to the goats to kill intestinal parasites and as a calcium supplement for their hooves. The way it works is that its microscopic sharp edges cut up parasite cell walls (this may help with Candida too), and its strong negative charge attracts heavy metals in the body and pulls them out. Silica is the main mineral (a semiconductor, like quartz sand, which may be why it helps with EMFs), and silica helps the body absorb calcium from the diet.

The negative charge seems to also make the body negatively charged, and to have a grounding effect on wireless radiation. I've found it is an amazing preventative to take before exposure. It may be one of the top things that has helped me. The cost, if you buy in bulk (Earthworks.com is where I get mine) is just pennies per day. Mix a teaspoon of diatomaceous earth in a full glass of water and drink on an empty stomach. I take it first thing in the morning or before town. It will help your hair and nails, and probably your bones and teeth too.

Example of Herbalism in Action:

I might bring, on a town trip, a coffee with mushroom mix and a jar of yarrow/red clover/chanca piedra tea with a spoonful of diatomaceous earth. Then, before bed that night, I'd make prickly lettuce tea with a scoop of mushroom mix and lion's mane tincture.

Harvesting Yarrow (Photo credit: Soula Marie)

Grounding

Forget about the New Age terminology and think about the real meaning of the word "grounded." The American Heritage Dictionary of the English Language (yes, I still use the dictionary) lists, as part of the definition of ground:
A. The position or portion of an electric circuit that is at zero potential with respect to the earth.
B. A conducting connecting to such a position or to the earth.
C. A large conducting body, such as the earth, as a return for electric currents and as an arbitrary zero of potential.

What this means is that electricity flows from positive to negative, and if you build up too much of a positive charge you can "ground it out" by standing on, yes, the ground. Lightning works this way. So does static electricity: you build up a positive charge by walking across the carpet, then you discharge it by shocking the negatively charged cat. You also build up a positive charge when you spend all day in town getting bombarded by wireless radiation. You discharge it by jumping into the river on the way home. Or walking barefoot on the dirt, or laying down on the ground. I've stopped scary, seizure-like nerve attacks this way.

Some people discharge excess charge by having a screaming fit at their family after excess wireless use. Ever notice how you feel calm and "neutral" after an emotional fit? Others choose a healthier approach by going for a run, which I've found can help use up some of the excess charge (barefoot is best).

Being positively charged is linked to diseases like high blood pressure, diabetes, and cancer. Being negatively charged is associated with good health and lots of energy (the New Agers had it backwards).

The good news is that being diligent about grounding after wireless exposure can keep even a severe electrosensitive alive and in good health for years. Gary swears by it, and says his use of grounding spoons, hot rocks, and sleeping on the ground speeds his recovery after town days. I have found this to be true as well.

The bad news (sorry) is that Elon Musk and others are in the process of deploying thousands of wireless communications satellites into the ionosphere, which will bathe Earth in a continuous fog of frequencies from which there will be no escape, even in the remotest of deserts. "Like a cell tower in the sky," in Elon's own words.

The good news (maybe? I'm a hopeless optimist) is that Gary is working on developing low-tech shielding technologies specific to satellite Wi-Fi, so that maybe it can buy us a little more time on Earth while we figure out how to get enough of the population to wake up to the fact that this insanity needs to stop.

Grounding Technologies

Spoons: You can thank Gary for this amazing low-tech version of expensive grounding equipment. You take a metal spoon, an insulated braided copper wire (can strip the rubber part off of old lamp cords for about three inches on each end-an electrician's wire-stripping tool is best, but you can use a knife), and a piece of copper rod a few inches long. Wrap one end of the copper wire around the end of the spoon, coiling it around several times and then securing it with electrical tape. Take the other end and wrap it around the copper rod. You now have a grounding spoon.

Stick the copper rod into the ground, pour water on it, then put the spoon on a part of your body that hurts, especially if it's a meridian point. Sit with this for at least a few minutes. I've run a cable from a grounding spoon out the window of my trailer, and I put the spoon against my skin when I sleep. Part of my evening routine is to go outside and pour a cup of water over the ground rod. This mimics the grounding effect of sleeping on the ground, but without the dirt and mosquitos.

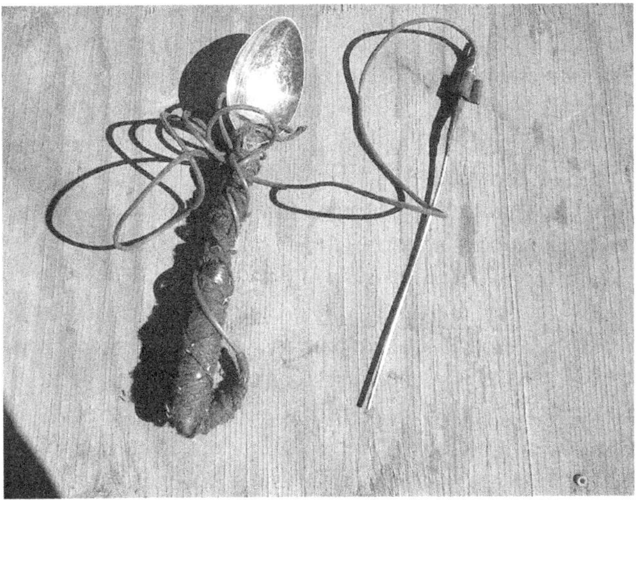

Hot Rocks:

A great way to heat up your bed in the winter, which also has grounding properties. Heat some round river rocks on top of the stove (a wood stove works best). Put these in your bed on cold winter nights. Make sure they are covered in something so you don't burn yourself. Also make sure that something is not polyester as it will melt and stink up the whole house (wool hats or socks work well).

Dirt Bags:

Put dirt in bags and pile around you when you sleep. Helps ground the body, but people may accuse you of sleeping with dirtbags.

Barefootin':

I was doing this before I even understood about electricity and grounding. It just feels right. I've built up callouses on my feet over the years (I even go barefoot in winter on a limited basis, such as walking out to the goat pen and back), so they're like an animal's paw pads. I rarely step on cactus or dog poop, because my feet just know where to go without me thinking about it (They're smarter than me, I joke). And if I do step on a cactus, I just pull it out and it doesn't hurt much because the skin is thick (dog poop is still icky).

Rubber soles stop the conduction of excess electricity

back into the ground; think about it, you're safe in a lightning storm in a car because of the rubber tires. Leather-soled moccasins work for grounding, but they are almost impossible to find. I had a pair once that I bought for eighty bucks, but I lost one in the woods while mushroom hunting.

Grounding on wet bare ground is best. You can pour some water onto a patch of ground and sit with your bare feet on the wet ground while reading a book or something.

Coating your body in mud: Messy, and you get some weird looks, but extremely grounding and helps block EMF, even when you're stuck in someone's backyard waiting for a ride out of town. Even just coating the backs of your hands and your forearms is helpful, as that area contains a lot of meridian endpoints.
Bentonite clay works well too and pulls out toxins, but mud is cheaper.

Sleeping on Ground:

Do this whenever possible. It can help you survive a high- EMF environment, or help you to get back to normal quicker after a town trip.

Epsom salts baths:

Magnesium is a calming, grounding mineral and absorbs into the skin when you bathe in it. Great for sore muscles and insomnia. I also make a liquid with dried magnesium citrate flakes and rub it on my skin. It can burn sensitive skin though.

Natural Hot Springs:

Even better. Electrosensitives love them.

Naked Sunbathing:

Great as it helps your body to produce Vitamin D (master hormone, great for everything), and provides near infrared light, which helps with structuring water in body. The more you sunbathe, the more you heal from EMF damage (just don't get burned, duh, and don't wear sunscreen, it blocks the frequencies that in this case you're trying to absorb and may contain toxic chemicals).

An added bonus is you can give the finger to whatever spy satellites might be watching.

The Day Everything Changed

June 13, 2017. I'm sitting in the waiting room at the hospital in Rutland, waiting for them to call me for my turn. I'm just here to get my blood drawn. The gastroenterologist next door sent me here, after our appointment. The pain in my gut has been bothering me and I still can't gain weight, and I have Medicaid now, so I've thought I should try to figure out what's up. My dad has come up from Connecticut to drive me to Rutland for the appointment. He's outside waiting in the car. The specialist said it sounded like I may have an ulcer. She's sent me to get my blood drawn, so she can try to figure it out. This should be a simple thing.

So I'm waiting in the Emergency Room, and it's taking forever, and they've given me a wireless buzzer that will light up and buzz when it's my turn. I don't like the thing so I've put it as far from me as I can on the end table. The whole place is making me feel awful. I'm getting a pounding headache, this pressure across my whole head. The air conditioned, disinfectant-smelling room is full of bored-looking people on their cellphones, punctuated by whining babies, annoying beeping noises, and other peoples' buzzers going off. I wish mine would go off. How long is this going to take?

I'm trying to read a magazine to get my mind off the headache. It's an article about Trump and Trump Tower, and how much money Trump has and how luxurious Trump Tower is. I'm imagining Trump sitting up there in Trump Tower, looking down at the city below and plotting how to make more money. The headache is getting worse. It feels like a vice grip now. I haven't had such a bad headache in a long time. Normally, I would leave a place if I felt this bad. But my dad has made a special trip to drive me here. And I need to get this stomach thing figured out. So tough it out, Julia, I think. I do have a high pain tolerance, I can handle this. Just deal with it, it will be over soon.

But the headache's getting worse and worse and has now reached the level of screaming pain. And I'm starting to feel it in the nerves of my arms, too, a prickling, and I'm getting this twitching in all of my muscles. I make my way up to the counter: is there any way they could get me in sooner, I inquire. I think I'm having a medical emergency, I tell them. The receptionist says no, I'll just have to wait. She looks bored. Never have a medical emergency in the Emergency Room. They don't care. Finally, the buzzer does go off and the nurse leads me into the exam room.

But at this point my muscles are spazzing uncontrollably and they say they're going to have to strap me down if they're to take my blood. And my vision's whiting out now, I can barely see. I finally wise up and realize, I've gotta get out of here NOW. I jump up from the chair and somehow make my way out of the hospital and into the bright sunshine. I can hardly see where I'm going and I end up running across the orange tape of a construction zone in the parking lot.

I find my dad's car, open the door and tell him, "I think I'm having a seizure." I run to a spot in the grass, where just an hour earlier I'd been showing him some mushrooms and edible plants, and lay down face first. I want to ground it out, this usually works for me. The pain is like nothing I've ever felt, like shards of broken glass cutting apart all the cells of my body, like waves that wash across my body and cause it to clench and spasm. It isn't exactly uncontrollable, and I don't think it's exactly a seizure; there's no loss of consciousness, and it's not like I'm shitting my pants or anything…but I have this urge to scream and smack the ground with my hands, so hard it hurts my hands.

"Fuck!!!!" I scream and hit the ground. "AHHHH!" Yelling seems to help the pain waves go through easier. "Goddamn Fuuuck! Growl!" I'm past caring if anyone is watching. However, I don't want my dad to worry, so I tell him I'm okay and give him a running commentary about what's happening, in between screams. It feels like I'm under psychic attack, like something's taken hold of my brain and I have to shake it off, to scream at it and make it go away. I growl, and I really am more angry than scared at this point. I'm ragingly angry. I'm also strangely calm and focused. This is what it's like, fighting an invisible enemy. I want to kill it like I did to my cell phone, but that's not possible. The attack can only happen one way.

After a point I realize it's over. Slowly, shakily, I get up. I walk to the car. No more pain waves. My vision is normal. The calm floods in and replaces the pain and anger. I can't even feel EMFs at all, at the moment. I take out a cinnamon stick from my backpack and chew it, as this lowers blood sugar and can sometimes help with the EMFs, and it further relaxes me.

"Well Dad," I say as we drive from the hospital's

parking lot, "You'll be happy to know I'm never going to hitchhike again. If that's a thing that can happen, I can't take the chance of it happening in a stranger's car, when I can't get out on the ground."

"Makes sense," he says.

The drive home is nice and I just look out the window at the scenery. My dad always has a calming presence. He doesn't freak out, and it's easy to not freak out when I'm around him. Maybe this is just a one time thing, I tell him.

Guess I shouldn't have tried to stay in the Emergency Room. Too bad the mission turned out to be a failure after all this.

At home, I cook some fish that my dad caught in Connecticut, and go to bed early in the shed. I feel fine all night.

The Invisible Fence

The next morning...I wake up in the shed and walk barefoot across the yard to the pool room door, so I can use the bathroom and make some coffee with the chaga tea that's in the crockpot. Bam! As soon as I walk into the house, it's like there's this wall of electricity. I feel it all. It's like prickling on my skin, my right eye twitching, sharp pains on the right side of my head. It's way worse than it's ever been. What the fuck. I quickly make the coffee and hurry back outside.

As I'm drinking my coffee and assessing the situation, I'm walking around the yard stomping out the bracken ferns that popped up yesterday. Zap! I get too close to the edge of the woods near the neighbor's yard, and it's like I hit an invisible fence. I walk toward the other neighbor's houses, stomping ferns along the way, and same thing, except for one house where I never see anyone and the Kindle hadn't detected any Wi-Fi. Only a small area around the shed, and the back porch of the house, feels okay.

Well, this is depressing, I think. What am I going to do now? I finish my coffee and do my best to go about my day, going for a walk down the railroad tracks and watering the garden, but I keep hitting the invisible fence wherever I go. My energy levels are pretty good, otherwise, but when I hit the invisible fence, I get a dizzy sense of disorientation and there are big blue veins on my arms that are bulging out and hurt when I'm around the electricity. I also notice there's a varicose vein on my left ankle that wasn't there yesterday. It's like a ropy blue knot, and looks like the veins my grandmother had. It hurts. What the fuck.

My dad's gone home and my brother is sleeping. There's no one I can talk to about this. Not that they would understand anyway. I try using the computer, and that is a mistake. It gives me a headache that puts me to bed for the next few hours. When I feel better, I'm hungry for dinner, so I go to the fridge to get out some meat to cook. Another mistake. The headache comes back and it takes a couple hours before I feel okay enough to even eat my dinner. I go to bed with a nasty headache and a stomachache. What the fuck.

Next morning, the invisible fence is still there. So are the varicose veins on my legs. I go for my hike, and as long as I stay away from houses that part of the day goes okay. But my own yard does not feel okay, and the house is pretty much off limits. I use the creek in the backyard as a way to keep food cool, like I did when I lived in the caves. The fire pit is fine for cooking, or my little camp stove. But it sucks that I can't even take care of my garden without getting zapped by the neighbors' Wi-Fi. The neighbors aren't even home this part of the year. It isn't fair that their radiation is polluting my territory.

Going out anywhere in the world, I soon find, is even worse. My brother leaves for a month to go touring with his band, and he lets me use his car while he's gone. So I finally have wheels to go exploring, but I find I can't get very far without feeling shaky and unsafe to drive. I go on some nature hikes and manage to be okay, but checking out coffee shops or antique stores or bookstores is a risky endeavor in which I have to keep a close watch on my levels of cognition to make sure I'm safe to drive home. Paradoxically, I'm wanting to be around people and civilization. I'm wanting to pretend things are normal, that they are the way they used to be. Why did I have to stay in the Emergency Room that long? I ask myself this question every day, many times a day. My life is divided into two parts: Before and After.

I go through a short phase in which I cope by getting drunk about it, like I did when I first became electrosensitive. I sip red wine from the bottle, which, mixed with the Saint Johnswort tincture I'm taking for the nerve pain, gives this euphoric glow to the mountains, the wildflower meadows of Queen Anne's lace and orange daylilies along the roadside, the Joe-Pye-Weed and orange hawkweed. It seems that the world has never been more beautiful. I wish I didn't feel like it was ending. I cry sometimes, laugh more often. I take a hike across a swinging bridge over a raging rapid stream somewhere along the Appalachian trail. I visit nurseries and buy potted plants. I blast an R.E.M. CD that I bought at a yard sale. Everywhere, there are power lines. Everywhere, I feel like I'm getting weaker. I know I'm going to have to stop going out into the world so much. But, it's just so beautiful…

What finally convinces me to stop fucking around with "the world" is when I attempt to take a road trip to see America's Stonehenge, an unexplained rock ruin in New Hampshire. I start getting a headache after the first few towns, but keep pushing onward anyway. When I get to Keane, New Hampshire, which sports a cell tower that looks like a tuning fork for giants, I start getting the shakiness in the nerves, the eye twitches and vision starting to go wonky. I know I need to get out of there and find woods, quick...I drive down the nearest backroad I can find, and keep driving, as far away from that cell tower as I can, down turn after turn of random backwoods roads. I don't feel safe driving and I know I have to find a spot to camp, but it's all private property here. Not much choice, though, unless I want to have a medical emergency.

I stop at a workshop/garage place on private land to see if I can find someone to explain the situation and ask if I can camp for the night. Seeing no one, I just keep driving until I come to a spot in the woods that looks like a summer camp or event venue. No one's there, so I pull off into a secluded space and lay down on the ground until the shakiness stops. Feeling better, I go for a walk in the oak and maple woodland. Squirrels and wild turkeys abound, and various mushrooms. I cook some meat on my camp stove, sleep in the back of the car, and in the morning I brew strong coffee, find the highway and get the fuck home. I was lucky, and quick-thinking in a crisis...but, that shit could have gone badly wrong. So I stop driving unless absolutely necessary.

I decide that I need to get a cat to help me deal with the loneliness. My neighbor drives me to the animal shelter, and I pick out a fat, bossy tortoiseshell named Sarah (or, she picks out me: she climbs in my lap and smacks any other cat who tries to get near me). Sarah sleeps in a cat bed next to me in the shed, and she quickly establishes the yard as her territory.

After awhile, with the symptoms not getting any better, I

decide that the best course of action is going to be for me to move to my family's other Vermont house, an abandoned house along the Mountain Road ski trail up Okemo Mountain. So I pack up my stuff and the cat, and drive the two miles up the Mountain Road to the upper house.

As I carry my stuff inside and set up my bed in the slate-floored foyer (the rest of the house is a mess and will need to be cleaned), the cat explores her new territory and I breathe in the scent of hemlock and fir trees and look out at the view of the Green Mountains. Wow, I think, at least I'm stranded somewhere beautiful. Never accept anything less than spectacular.

Fritillary Butterfly (Photo credit: Soula Marie)

The Abandoned House

The reason the Mountain Road house is abandoned is that, after my grandfather built it in the early 90's, he was unable to get an easement from Okemo to build a road to the house. The Mountain Road is drivable in the summer months, but in winter it turns into a ski trail, and the only way to get to the house is to ski to it. This wasn't practical for a house to live in, and my grandfather (famous for his stubbornness, and probably the genetic origin of my own stubbornness) never gave up the fight, with the result that the house sat abandoned for decades while Grandfather fought his legal battle.

The main construction of the house was done, and it's like a miniature version of the main house, with beautiful wood paneling and black and white marble tiled bathrooms. But it wasn't ever finished, the floors were still not done and the electrical wiring was never finished (which was just fine with me). There's running water from the well, but you have to go down into the basement and fill a bucket from a spigot. The toilets flush if you use a bucket of water. There's no kitchen stove, but there is a propane burner set up. There's a fireplace with marble tile, like the one at the main house.

For years, friends and family had stopped here while skiing to take a break and have some tea or hot chocolate. One time, when I was in my late twenties, I had even spent a month living here in the winter, because my grandfather was driving me nuts and I wanted to get away from him. Also, I'd wanted to test my survival skills. I spent a lot of time running up and down the stairs to stay warm, as there wasn't any firewood and the snow was too deep to go out and cut any.

I'd tried to start a bow drill fire (unsuccessfully), and tried to snare snowshoe hares in the snowy woods (also unsuccessfully). Since then, vandals had stolen the copper pipes out of the wall and also stolen an antique wood-burning stove, and smashed some windows. Garbage and pink fiberglass insulation are all over the basement, and the rest of the house isn't much better.

So I get to work cleaning the house, and it is good because it gives me a mission and some structure to my days. Up here without any electricity and barely within cell phone reception, I almost can forget about being electrosensitive. It feels good to be doing meaningful work and not just sick all the time. But any time I leave "the island" and get within range of any Wi-Fi, I get a brutal reminder of just how limited my world is now.

There's times when I'm out hiking the ski slopes with Sarah- the cat will follow me anywhere- and I'll accidentally get too close to the "invisible fence" of Wi-Fi that surrounds each of the ski lodges. Instantly, I'll have no energy and my legs won't even want to do the work to carry me home. I have to practically drag myself home, or lay down in the moss for awhile until my energy comes back. I also am careful to avoid humans, because my sense of smell has gotten stronger and one whiff of artificial fragrance can knock me down as bad as electricity. So if I'm hiking on a trail, I go off to the side as far as I can get when I hear people coming. That way I won't have to smell them.

I swear I'm feeling airplanes too, the small sightseeing planes that fly around the National Forest. When I hear one coming, I say, "Death from above!" And dive down onto the forest floor, grounding, try to make a game of it. It's not actually fun though. I also avoid cars, walking through the woods instead of up the road when I'm going to one of my favorite hiking spots. I have a sizable territory here on this one area of the mountain that happens to be mostly blocked from cell tower signals. It's on the side of Okemo, but in kind of a crack between Okemo and Jackson Peak, and there are no other houses nearby. There is a large Satan tree directly on top of Okemo, but I'm out of range of it here, and luckily there is no tower on top of Jackson. The nearest Wi-Fi would be that of Jackson Lodge, but that is a couple ski trails away. I feel like an endangered species on a wildlife reserve.

Part of my tiredness is from not eating enough, because my stomach (or whatever it is, going back to the hospital is not an option) is always acting up and I'm nauseous all the time. I'm never sure what's okay to eat, root vegetables usually work, and toasted buckwheat, and eggs, and coconut oil. I also have some baker's chocolate bars, and some bags of dried liver from a local farm (technically, these are dog treats, but they taste great). I gather wild greens too, but it's limited what I can find within the invisible fence. Milkweed greens and a few dandelion leaves are about all there is, except on rare occasions when I walk down to the main house and forage what's left of my abandoned garden.

I take a look at myself in the mirror of the black-and-white marble tiled bathroom and think, I'm looking old and scrawny. Dark circles under my eyes. It seems so long since age 27 when I was here just to test my survival skills, when the only problem I had to hide from was my grandfather. Well, I guess I did turn out to be good at surviving. Not so fucking fun now that it's real, now is it, Julia? Well...I grin at myself in the mirror...sometimes it's fun. I haven't lost my fighting spirit yet. Here in my crumbling mansion, alone on a mountainside in this one spot that's somehow, serendipitously, eluded the ravages of the mechanized world...drinking mate among the blackberry brambles and broken glass...hiding from cars and airplanes...life is strange. You really *never* do know where you're going to end up.

I listen to a lot of NPR. There's Science Friday, Wait, Wait Don't Tell Me, BBC News. I have Vermont and New Hampshire NPR to choose from. No other stations. The radio's on all the time, and those irritating monotone voices are kind of my sanity, until one day, I notice the familiar nerve twitching whenever I go in the kitchen where the radio is. I ignore this for a couple days- no, please, not my one link with the outside world- but it becomes too obvious, and I have to turn it off. Then it's just my own voice and the cat for company.

The cat and I get in arguments sometimes. She is an obnoxious roommate, screaming at her full food dish to tell me it's not good enough. I tell her shut the fuck up, leave me alone, go hunt mice, and she sulks off to "her" room, one of the upstairs bedrooms. My room is now the downstairs bathroom. It's small and cozy, and I feel that the marble is an extra layer of protection against cars with Wi-Fi that drive by on the Mountain Road. Also, it feels like there's less cell signal the lower down I am. I have a foam pad and sleeping bag on the floor between the toilet and the shower.

What drives me the most nuts is that, although I'm exhausted and spend a lot of time in bed, my mind is working great and I'm desperate to be learning.
Going to the library is out of the question. Mostly, I read and reread my mushroom books. There's also this book of poetry that I walk around reading out loud sometimes. Once or twice a tourist wanders into the yard and I don't mind at all, I even give them a tour of the house, because even hermits need a certain amount of human interaction. I read my field guides at night- the one to eastern butterflies provides hours of entertainment- but I do have to conserve my candle supply. I have some little tea lights that I found in a drawer of the main house, unscented, of course. No amount of darkness would ever convince me to light a Yankee candle.

When autumn comes and the sugar maples set the hillside ablaze with brilliant color, my dad has a cord of wood delivered so I can make fires in the fireplace. Some of the logs are covered with beautiful polypore mushrooms, and I set my favorite ones aside as display pieces for awhile before burning them. The polypores are some of the most beautiful things in nature, I believe. I spend hours every evening watching the fire, and listening to books on CD that my mom brought, a rare luxury. It gets cold enough to use two sleeping bags on the bathroom floor. I know my days here in the sanctuary are drawing to an end.
I wonder what it would be like to spend a winter up here? I'd have to better insulate an area of the house,

maybe build something up around the fireplace. It would be cold. I wish I had building skills. I could hike up supplies in a backpack like I did when I stayed here before, or my family could deliver things by skiing here. At least refrigeration wouldn't be an issue. If I was twenty pounds heavier and in better shape, I would seriously consider doing this. It might even be fun.
But being this skinny and in this poor health, I feel that it would be too risky and irresponsible to try to survive the ten and twenty degree average nighttime temperatures up here in the winter.

But I don't want to leave. I wait until November, when the first snow of the year is falling, before I hike down and get Max to come up with the car and help me move. We pack up all my stuff and the cat, and we're just in time, as Okemo's staff has just roped off the Mountain Road and we have to get them to let us through. I carry my books and clothing and bedding into the main house- there isn't much- and the electricity feels alien, buzzy, as soon as I get in the door. The florescent lights are overpowering bright, and there's the noise of the fridge, and the smell of artificial fragrances. My brother's music on the stereo is nice though, and there are many books I haven't read yet. I try to decide where in the house will be the lowest EMF area to sleep, finally deciding on the upstairs sun room.

That first night, the headache is bad. My heart is racing, my veins hurt, and I'm wondering if I'm even going to survive the night. I reach a place within myself where I'm not attached to the outcome. I know I've done the best I possibly can, and that will have to be good enough. What more can I do? After a few hours, the attack does stop, and I actually feel bored, and hungry. I go down to the root cellar to get something to eat. Then I sleep well through the rest of the night. One night down, six months more to go.

Chaga Dreams

A side effect of mega dosing on chaga and cat's claw the whole time I was in Vermont was that I was experiencing vivid lucid dreams almost nightly. Many of them dealt with post Apocalyptic or dystopian future themes, or TV or media of some kind. It was so entertaining at times that it made up for the long hours of boredom during the day. Who needs TV with dreams like these? Here are some of the most memorable.

The Creepy Arm Guy

(Years later, I still crack up laughing when I think of this one, although it was really annoying when it was happening).

"I'm on a bus with a bunch of people, and there's this app people can get for their phones to play a practical joke on their friends. What you do is you use the app is to point to a specific person, and then whenever that person happens to ask what time it is, this hologram of an old, smelly, creepy, drunk guy staggers over to the unfortunate victim, gets all up in your personal space and breathes all over you, just keeps coming at you...and then he dangles his limp, dead arm in your face. And on his arm is a watch, with the correct time.
Anyway, since I was the only one without a cell phone on the bus, I would ask someone what time it was and the old drunk guy would stagger over and dangle his arm in my face. It was annoying and kind of awful while it was happening, and everyone on the bus found it hilarious. After awhile I would forget and ask what time

it was again, and the whole thing would happen over again."

The Giraffe Movie

"A commercial comes on about a new comedy movie starring a CGI talking giraffe. The giraffe has escaped from the zoo in New York, and he's on his way to Hollywood to become a movie star. What's funny is that, once he puts on a suit and tie, the people don't notice he is a giraffe, they just think he is a really tall human (Kids notice, but their parents just tell them it's not polite to point at people). The giraffe has a sarcastic personality and is kind of an asshole.

There's this bridge that's under construction, and the giraffe wants to walk under it but he doesn't feel like bending down, so he pulls a lever and the whole bridge comes crashing down. Then he lets out this ridiculous, dorky laugh- HA HA HA!- and does this expressive move with his neck along with the laugh, and that's the conclusion of the commercial."

he Zombie Apocalypse

"I'm outside in a suburban neighborhood, when all of a sudden I feel a pulse go out across the wireless networks. The crows stop cawing, all birdsong stops, and a quiet chill creeps across the lawns. I get a headache and feel shitty, but am otherwise unaffected. But the people around me are changed. They act like something is attacking them, and then they succumb to it and start attacking each other like zombies.

My brother is trying to fight it off, he has enough awareness to tell me to go in the house and lock the door. I do, and my mom is inside. She is strangely unaffected (maybe her cell phone was off that day?), but she also seems completely oblivious to what is going on. When my cousin staggers up to the door, obviously a zombie, my mom goes to the door to open it even though my brother and I are screaming at her not to. Then I wake up."

The Brain Chip

(This one was years before I'd ever heard of Neuralink, and it still gives me chills to think about it)

"I'm in a classroom with a group of my peers. There are friends from Moab along with people from my high school and even way back in elementary school, and people I don't recognize from real life but that I seem to know in the dream. Everyone knows each other and this seems to be normal. We're all about high school age. We're sitting at desks, those kind we had in school where the chair is built into the desk.

Anyway, my friends are all excited because tomorrow's the day when they'll all be able to get a chip in their heads so they can merge with AI and be able to be connected with each other through the Internet. They're all whispering excitedly about how cool it will be that they'll be able to link minds and have superpowers and be all together.

"Well, not all of us are going to do it..." Someone

whispers. They all look over at me, a little guiltily. I stand up at my desk, and I give a speech. It is the most show of emotion most of them have ever seen from me, and the words flow effortlessly and come from the heart.

"Friends," I tell them, "This is not what you think it is. The AI wishes to become conscious. It wants to know what it is like to have bodies, to experience the world from a human point of view. You may think you're getting superpowers, but you will be giving up your humanity forever. You may think you're still you, but it won't be you looking out from your eyes anymore. It will be looking out from your eyes. You will be gone. The AI will be all that's left. Please don't do this."

I sit back down. Many of my friends are crying. They know at some level that what I say is true. But they know they're going to do it anyway."

The Long Winter

When I was a kid, one of the games we'd play in my grandfather's house was Don't Touch the Hot Lava. I think all kids play some version of this game. We'd jump from bed to bed, or climb across various pieces of furniture, trying to avoid the "hot lava" that was the floor.

Well, I'm 35 years old now, and I'm in my grandfather's house again, in those same rooms, playing a real life version of Don't Touch the Hot Lava. In this version, it's Don't Touch the Electric Field, and the stakes are higher now. The goal is to avoid getting zapped as much as possible, so I can get through the winter still alive and with minimal nerve damage. I've found if I am careful, I actually can get through a day without feeling too bad.

But it takes strategy. It's like a chess game. I can't just stomp around the house like the rest of my family, no, I have to plan my moves. I must have infinite patience. I must not feel sorry for myself and say "fuck it," because doing that could cause nerve damage I can't afford right now. There is no room at all for self pity. None. Not even when I have to lay in bed for hours staring at the wall. Stay within the safe zones (there aren't many). Wait. Dream.

A typical day is, I wake up in my room, the second room upstairs. I've moved to this room because we realized it was the one room to which we can turn off the electric breaker without it affecting anything else essential (although it does turn off half the outlets in the rooms on either side). My room, a casual observer might notice, has all the furniture crowded into only half the room. This is because the other half is electrified (I don't know whether it's from the neighbor's Wi-Fi or the electric wires in the house's walls). They also might notice that my bed is pulled away from the wall about three feet. This is because, if the power is turned on (as we have to do, on weekends when there are Airbnb guests in the room next door) then I want to be away from the walls.

So, the first thing I do when I wake up, is I walk across the room into the electric zone, and dump the pee bucket out the window into the snowbank (no one goes over there in winter anyway). Then I grab my backpack, which last night I've packed with all the essential things I might want with me for the day- herbal remedies, warm clothes, whatever book I'm currently reading, notebook and pencil, watch, last night's dinner dishes, and whatever garbage I might have (cans, wrappers or whatever). Prepared for the day, I run down three sets of stairs, a spiral staircase spiraling down to the basement, to the safest bathroom. While I'm there, I also do my dishes in the sink (as the kitchen is definitely off limits). I brush my teeth and get ready for the day.

After that I run up one flight of stairs into the downstairs sunroom. This area, which also includes a small couch in the middle part of the living room, is one of the safest areas of the house and the place where I spend the most time besides my bedroom. I keep my camp stove in here usually. This early in the morning, there's usually no one around who would think it is weird that I'm using the camp stove to heat up water for my Yerba mate. I have a little herbal medicine shelf in here with various herbs in jars, and organizing and reorganizing them is one source of entertainment. I drink mate and sit in the chair, looking out at the snowy woods. Typically, I'll read for awhile, usually an herbal book or mushroom book, or one of the hundreds of National Geographics we have in the house. I'll try to entertain myself as long as possible before I can't take it anymore and I have to go do something.

Usually, that means a walk, and so, instead of using the front door where there is a lot of electricity, I run down the stairs to the basement, grab my coat and boots from the hall closet, and then go up the cold, concrete stairs that lead to the side door of the house. I first make sure there isn't a giant icicle hanging overhead waiting to impale me, and if there isn't, I go outside into the yard. The driveway's pretty safe, but I hurry past the houses, which all have Wi-Fi.

When I come to the cul-de-sac at the end of Mountain View Road, I know I'm safe, and I go into the woods. There I can hike as long as I want and not feel any electricity, as I explore among the hemlocks and look for chaga and follow tracks of deer and bobcat. This was my safe place when I was a kid too, and I had such a sense of freedom here even though school was always looming at the end of the weekend. It was the bluest sky I ever remember, those winter days. Well, school's out forever, I console myself. I'm fighting for my life now…but at least I don't have to worry about that math test.

It is cold and the snow is deep, so eventually I don't want to walk anymore, and I head back toward the house. I go in through the basement door and usually go back to my spot on the couch. Usually I'm hungry by then, so I might cook some buckwheat and eggs on the camp stove, or maybe I've put some meat in the crockpot before I left. I keep my spices in the puzzle cupboard in the living room. Usually, there's other people around by then, and if I'm lucky someone may wander over into my little corner of the world and talk to me.

The biggest problem with people being around is they are always using the microwave, which I swear I can feel even though it's supposed to be insulated. I keep an eye on whatever humans are around, since sooner or later I know they're going to use it. As soon as I hear those annoying beeps, I take off running to the door, barefoot across the snowy driveway to the mailbox. No mail today, oh well. I take my time and walk back to the house. Keeps my feet tough. Or I have the option of running to the downstairs bathroom. I may choose that time to take a shower (and do my lunch dishes in the shower).

People also use their cell phones a lot, so I make myself scarce if that is happening near me. And occasionally someone will smell so badly of artificial fragrances (luckily with my brother that's not a problem, he uses Dr. Bronner's for his weekly shower) that I'll have to go up to my room to get away from them.

Luckily, adrenaline seems to have a cancelling effect on getting "zapped," and so does the running. Sometimes if I get too much electricity, it will give me a jolt of energy and I'll just go out for a run until I don't feel it anymore. It's kind of like doing really bad drugs. Showering also seems to help with the EMFs (and is something to do).

The worst is if I get zapped during or after a meal, because it throws off digestion and makes my stomach hurt, so I try to plan meals around when I won't need to leave the safe spots for awhile. Sometimes I gain a couple pounds and it feels like I'm getting ahead. Other times, I lose weight and feel discouraged.

Cleaning the house for Airbnb guests is something to do once a week, but it does take me into parts of the house where there is an electric field, so I do it in the mornings on days when I am feeling at my best, and well caffeinated. Luckily the upstairs isn't as bad as the downstairs for EMFs, and I can usually handle it okay, as long as Max deals with Roomba.

The hardest times are weekends, when there are Airbnb guests and I have to turn on the power to my room so the guests next door won't be in the dark. I can't sleep in my room with the power turned on. It's scary, I can feel the headaches and "prickly" feeling in my arms, the swelling in my lymph glands. So I sleep in Max's car on weekends. It's actually comfortable, if I use two sleeping bags and a lot of blankets. He parks it in a dark corner of the yard in a spot where guests won't notice. A few times when it's extra cold, I sleep on the floor in the downstairs bathroom, getting up before dawn so no one notices. Sometimes I also cook my dinner in here, if there's guests around and I don't want them to see me cooking on the camp stove in the sunroom.

Somehow I make it through six months of winter with my sanity and physical health intact. I've lived in caves, been in mental institutions, hitchhiked all over America, and had all kinds of adventures in my life. But that long winter in my family's house was one of the hardest experiences I've ever gone through.

I'm glad I did it. I feel changed, like it was an initiation. I'm older, more patient now, not so easily phased. I know it's time to go back to Moab. I pack up all my essentials and some food in my backpack and buy an Amtrak ticket.

The Amtrak

Somewhere in Nebraska, on a long stretch of track with nothing but cornfields as far as the eye can see, the train stops moving. I wait, along with all the other passengers, squirming in our uncomfortable seats. Is there something wrong with the train? We wait some more. The staff is nowhere to be found. It's like they all just bailed and left us here. Minutes turn to hours, and still no word on why we're still sitting here. The Lysol smell gets stronger, and I can feel electrical fields from peoples' various devices. People are texting furiously, and starting to grumble amongst themselves.

I walk down to the lower level and find that a group of smokers has opened a window (which we're not allowed to do) so they can smoke cigarettes out the window. I join them, and take turns going over to the window to take breaths of fresh air.

"What the fuck is going on?" I ask.

"I heard something about terror threats," says one lady.

"I heard they're having a shift change and they messed up on their hours and can't get another crew yet," says a young guy with a bandana who's smoking Marlboro's.

I hang out with the smokers for awhile, until without warning the lady sprays perfume all over herself and I have to stop breathing and run upstairs. Upstairs, tempers are high, and one lady is shouting. Finally, a sheepish-looking staff member shows up, and one of the passengers, Carl, demands he bring us water, which he eventually does: tiny bottles of water, enough for us each to have one, and a stale-looking cookie for everyone too. Carl takes them and distributes them to everyone. I give the cookie to the kid in the seat behind me.

"Snacks and bottled water are available for purchase in the cafe," a voice on the intercom informs us. Fuck you, I think. I end up spending about twenty dollars on water during this layover. I'm running low on food, since I packed so minimally, but I'm going to just have to suffer on that one. No way am I eating their poisoned, overpriced shit.

Headaches, inflammation, can't breathe. As the hours go by, this is ever more difficult. I'm looking outside at the blue sky, the sunflowers, the long stretch of highway, and I can see all the fresh air blowing through the cornstalks. Maybe I should just hitchhike the rest of the way. It would be risky too, but at least it would be proactive.

I squeeze down the narrow stairway with my backpack to the luggage rack where my main, huge backpack is. I'm going to have to get rid of some of my stuff if I'm going to be able to carry all this. It sucks, but stuff is easier to replace than brain cells. I manage to take off about thirty pounds of unneeded weight and bulk: camping gear, books, clothes. But then a voice announces that we are experiencing problems with the shift change, but that the train should be up and running in three more hours. I decide to wait.

But now I'm feeling lightheaded and dizzy from not

eating, and I realize I need to do something about it so I don't pass out. It's not about being uncomfortable, it's reached to point of being a survival situation, so I decide to reevaluate the food options. I sit in the booth seat in the cafe car, and scrutinize the menu. Mostly it's stuff like ham sandwiches, scrambled eggs, burritos, bags of chips. I know that gluten would make me sick and might even kill me under these circumstances (and spending the rest of the day in the train's cramped, chemical-smelling bathroom, shitting my guts out a hundred times while the rest of the passengers pound angrily on the door, does not sound fun). I'm willing to chance something non-organic, because I know that pesticide damage, for me, is more of a long-term problem, not an acute immediate danger (Let the future take care of itself). But is there even anything on this damn menu without gluten?

It's at this point I actually break down and start crying. Days of no sleep, chemical and electrical torture and near starvation have brought me to a breaking point. I'm embarrassed, and try to hide the tears, but it ends up working in my favor because the lady at the counter takes pity on me. She says I can have a bowl of plain oatmeal, and two oranges, on the house. I eat these and now have renewed energy to face the rest of this trip. I go back to my seat.

By this point I haven't slept in three days, and I've been taking strong herbs the whole time (pretty much everything on my list, all mixed together), and the result is that I'm almost tripping. I close my eyes and watch the hoofbeats of the buffalo beating the earth like a drum, reverberating into the atmosphere as thunder and calling down the rain. In Denver I see into the future and watch dark armies of cyborgs marching across the plains. Finally, still alive and much worse for wear, I stumble off the train in Green River and hitch to Moab, where my friend Kurt says I look terrible and gives me a ride to The Land.

The Land, this desert: the place that gets into your blood and makes you too crazy to live anywhere else. I lay down in the red dirt, kiss the ground, and tell my friends, "Remind me never to leave here again."

Desert Rat Hits Rock Bottom

Maybe its my own increased self-confidence gained from the Vermont ordeal, but I'm no longer feeling like everyone thinks I'm crazy. Back on The Land, which has a new rotating cast of characters who live here part-time in trailers, I feel like a minor celebrity, returning to the desert. Jack gives me an empty camper to stay in, and everyone seems happy that I am here (Myrtle especially). I teach people about how to cook tumbleweeds and how to make wild mustard sauerkraut. I go for long walks through the greasewood and sagebrush, and spend hot afternoons reading in the cool spaces under rocks.

One day at the base of Predator Tower with a couple new friends, I ask them to turn off their phones and they say, "No problem," and turn them off. They don't seem all that surprised that some people can react badly to electronics. It seems like this is becoming more common knowledge these days. Pretty much everyone I tell about my electrosensitivity now seems to get it. Town is more of a hellhole than ever, but I just don't go there. I spend over a month out here recovering. My nervous system feels like it is finally getting some rest.

Unfortunately I agree to housesit in Castle Valley for Jack's mom, and a month with a Smartmeter is a month too long. The house is a historic homestead which includes three dugout shelters, used by early settlers to store supplies, and I sleep in one of these (originally the meat house), to stay protected against Castle Valley's new towers. I unplug the Wi-Fi and the refrigerator, and stay outside often, but it's still too much. By the end of the month I'm more sensitive, and any good I've done with my month on The Land has been reversed. And it's too hot now to be at The Land.

Back to the caves at Mill Creek. It's July and the sand is so hot it actually scorches my feet to run across it at midday. Sometimes Kurt hikes up to visit me, brings me care packages of coconut yogurt and coconut butter, hangs out with me on the beach by Emerald pool. It's nice to know that someone cares, it means a lot.

Mostly I'm alone and I settle into a comfortable routine. I sleep on the cool dirt floor of the caves, wake up at sunrise and drink cold brew Yerba mate from my cooking pot. During the day, I make chaga tea by putting it in a mason jar and setting it out in the sun. I alternate between "Haunted Cave" and "Pirate Cave" mostly, and have buried stashes of food and cooking pots in both. Midday, I read on the beach by Emerald Pool, jump in, lay back in the sun. It would feel like paradise if I didn't feel so sick.

Problem is, whatever's wrong with my stomach is really wrong now, and its hard to eat anything without my guts swelling up so bad it makes me almost cry. It feels like a hard lump, like something's stuck in there, and eating exacerbates the problem. I go as long as I can without food to avoid the pain.

I'm never really sure what is okay to eat, either, and I spend way too much time walking to town to load up my backpack with supplies. Canned sardines, coconut oil, coconut yogurt, avocados, seaweed, and goat yogurt are some of the things I buy (luckily, I do have food stamps). I hitchhike out of the parking lot to avoid the "walk of shame" (a stretch of main road where it's obvious, if you're walking down this road with a backpack, that you're living up the canyon, which is illegal these days), and then I walk along the bike path and past a lot of cell towers to go shop at Moonflower, which has some of the worst Wi-Fi in town.

By the time I make it back up the canyon by evening, my nerves are fried and I'm starving, and I'll eat a bunch of food and then spend the next day with a horrible stomachache and feeling shaky.

One day, while bathing in the creek with my shorts and shirt on in order to accomplish a bath and laundry at the same time, I realize I can feel every vertebrae and my hip bones are sticking straight out. I'm so tired, I think, it's hard to even stand up. I'm out of food, and I think if I don't go get some today I might not actually be able to walk out of here tomorrow. I don't want to walk to town. It's so long, and the Wi-Fi is so bad. It's a sobering realization. But I have to go, and I pull myself up and start moving. And I glide down the trail, effortlessly and it feels wonderful. It's like I'm being powered by something that isn't me. The cottonwoods shimmer green along the creek below me, and the sky is blindingly beautiful blue above. Is this even real? What a strange dream my life is these days.

I hear things, visualize things this summer that aren't of this world. Weird dreams in the Haunted Cave. Visions under alien-looking petroglyphs of strange horned figures. I think it's because I'm so close to other side myself, the veil is thin. Or else I'm finally, actually, losing my shit due to malnutrition. Or both.

Rock bottom is on my 36th birthday, alone in Pirate Cave, grabbing my stomach and groaning in pain and yelling at God to just kill me. "Or, you could just fix it," I say calmly as an aside, "That would be okay too."

A Serendipitous Meeting

Of all the various food items that I shop for at Moonflower, it is the goat yogurt that I feel is most helpful to me. It's pasteurized, though, which makes it harder to digest, and I know raw goat milk and yogurt would help me more. I know this because I used to do yard work for a couple in Castle Valley who had goats, and I'd sometimes buy milk from them. I have this sense that goat milk is exactly what my body needs to heal itself.

Problem is, you can't find raw milk products on the shelf at Moonflower, because it is illegal to sell it commercially. You have to know a farmer personally. One day I'm talking with another customer at Moonflower about goat milk, and the store's manager happens to overhear me.

"You know," he says, "I have a friend in Colorado who has goats. I should connect you with her. She's into herbalism and has a lot of sensitivities herself, you two would really get along and she'd probably tell you to come live with her."

He arranges for us to meet (as I can't use a phone myself to call her), and a few days later at Moonflower's member party I meet up with Soula in the store's crowded deli. There are bowls of free samples along the store's aisles, music blares from the loudspeakers, and many people I know from the town are here, all of them trying to talk to me at once. A slim, pretty middle-aged woman wearing flower-patterned pants, a felt hat and turquoise earrings, Soula seems as stressed by the chaos of our surroundings as I am. "Let's go outside," she shouts over the noise.

"Sounds good," I shout, and I follow her outside to the purple bench in front of the store near the planter full of Datura plants (we both position ourselves away from the Smartmeter, I notice). We talk about our interests, herbalism and gardening, and I tell Soula about how I'm Wi-Fi sensitive and living in a cave.

"I'm sensitive too," she says. "We turned on Wi-Fi last year, and I felt like I had the flu for a whole month, could barely get out of bed at all, and my beehives died…and I'd be outside vomiting, and there would be all these dead bees, and I'd wonder if there was a connection. Finally I figured it out and I unplugged the Wi-Fi, and I got better. Instantly. And the bees came back."

"Wow," I say.

"Yeah," says Soula. "You should come live at my place. It would be good to have another person here who's sensitive so I can have some backup when the guys tell me it's all in my head."

"I'm pretty sick sometimes," I say. "I want to not be a burden…but I'm a hard worker, I can help in the garden, I'll make sure to help out."

"There's a camper you can stay in," Soula says. "And I can help you out with food, and try to figure out what herbs to use to heal your problems."

"Awesome," I say. We arrange to meet up again in a few days, after I've gone to the hospital to get my endoscopy. It feels great to finally have a plan, a glimpse of hope. And the goat cheese sample Soula gives me is amazing and agrees with my stomach...I want more of that.

Soula later tells me that her friends at Moonflower had warned her of the possibility that I might drop dead on her and she'd been a bit concerned about this as well, but that then I'd made some joke and she'd thought, well, maybe this girl is going to be okay.

The Hospital

I'm at the hospital, calm and dozy-feeling because I've just taken a big shot of chamomile tincture, about to go under anesthesia for an endoscopy/ colonoscopy. The hospital smells like chemicals and all around me, various Dark Force Machines are humming and beeping. The hardest part was actually getting my shit together to schedule this procedure: making the phone calls (Bob at the coffeeshop lets me use his landline), going to the preliminary appointments, going for the Ultrasound where they took pictures of my digestive organs. Then a day of fasting and Epsom salts yesterday, and shitting in a hole in the sand in the desert all day and feeling like I'm about to pass out, and black coffee this morning and how nice it was that Jack drove me here, and finally I'm going to get this thing resolved.

The fear, of course, is not of the procedure itself but of the hospital. I don't want a repeat of my experience at the hospital in Rutland. But I'm smarter now, and I always come here dosed up on various nerve-relaxant herbs (and today the residual effect of the Epsom salts, which is magnesium, is also helping).

The nurse puts an IV in my arm with the anesthetic, and the next thing I remember I'm awake and rubbing my eyes and saying, "Is it over?" It was. I'm still alive. And it's over. This is the biggest sense of relief I've felt in a long time, and I wander outside to sit a bench in the sunshine under a desert willow and I still feel kind of woozy and happy.

Turns out, as I find out a couple weeks later when I get my results, it was my gallbladder all along. My stomach is pretty much fine, except for some mild ulceration. But my gallbladder's fucked up and full of sludge, and they recommend I take it out (I tell them I'll think about it). I also have a horrible Candida infection of the esophagus, which the doctor says could be life- threatening if I don't take antibiotics (which is pretty stupid since antibiotic use is a cause of Candida in the first place). Modern medicine is great for diagnosis.

Now that I know what's wrong, I can figure out what natural remedies to take to fix it.

The Farm

Soula meets me again at Moonflower, and this time she's here with her son Jess, in an old blue pickup, full to the top of watermelons, and with a cat in a carrier who's just been spayed. Jess talks a mile a minute, and has blond hair sticking out in different directions, and he and Soula drive around selling watermelons to everyone they meet. I'm squeezed in between them, with my backpack and bags somehow stuffed in the spaces between the watermelons, and I'm eating crackers with goat cheese and thoroughly enjoying the whole scene. They both know so much. Ecuadorian herbs, biodynamic preparations, minerals to add to soil, how to grow the best vegetables. I have this sense, looking out at miles of empty desert and tumbleweeds and sagebrush, like we're back in pioneer times and this is my family, I'm supposed to be here now.

The farm is in a hidden corner of a town that's also off the beaten path. A quarter mile of rough dirt track leads to the entrance. Two big friendly dogs, Blue and Tiger Lily, greet us at the entrance. A rough wooden fence surrounds an orchard paradise, with about fifty varieties of fruit trees, several greenhouses and outbuildings, a straw bale house where Jess lives, a couple campers, a small house covered in solar panels where Soula lives. Goats baaaa from their pens, chickens poke around looking for bugs, several Manx cats compete for my attention. I settle into my camper and begin a new chapter in my life.

Although it is off-grid and far from the electromagnetic

Hell of civilization, the farm has its own electrical problems. I soon realize that the field put out by Soula's inverter (which converts the harmless DC from the solar panels into jagged, chaotic AC waveforms that supply the farm's power) affects me as badly as Wi-Fi if I get anywhere near the house. Soula manages to find me enough to do in places out of its range- weeding the onion beds in the orchard, or planting baby sagebrushes along the fence, for example- but in order to do what I've come here for, which is to learn about goats, I sometimes have to go within the inverter's range.

On my second day here, I'm washing out water buckets, about as simple a job as you can get, and yet I'm having trouble figuring this out. Why is everything so hard? I flash back to life in my teens and early 20's: not being able to concentrate at school, getting lost on the way to work. I was a good dog walker and weed puller back then. Anything more complex, such as entering numbers in a cash register, forget it- it was like there was some kind of delay in reception between my brain and the rest of the world. It sucked, and this sucks too. I resolve to focus through the pain and brain fog so I can stay on task. Mind over matter. I somehow manage to finish the buckets.

I can't even find my way around the farm, and take wrong turns constantly. Where's the apple tree today? Certainly not in the same place it was yesterday, that would be too easy. I can't go in the house either, because of the electricity. I use a long stick to tap on the door if I need to ask Soula a question. I feel left out, like I'm just some bum living in the backyard, doing whatever chores I can to survive.

Soula, of course, doesn't want me to feel this way, and she's always coming out to my camper to bring me millet pancakes, or cheese, or just to hang out. We take a drive up into the mountains to gather acorns, which I process and she cooks into Umitas (a form of corn tamale). She shows me how to strain duff and goat poop through a metal screen and mix them together to make soil from the garden. She gives me pears to cut up and dry on drying racks in the sun. She tells me which weeds I can cut to feed to the goats, and is impressed by the fact that I know the plants as well as she does. Soula seems to get it that my brain just doesn't work sometimes; she says don't worry about it and just find something you can do and focus on the good things.

"I'm so glad you came here," she says.
"Me too," I say. "I just wish that inverter wasn't here."

One day Soula and I are mulching the green onion beds with hay from the goat pens, and we both have headaches and feel spacey and jittery from the inverter. I might have to leave here soon because of it, I think sadly. I wish the inverter would just die.

Soula gets up and goes into the house for something. She comes back in a panic because the inverter's smoking and making a loud buzzing noise. "I think it's fried," she says. "What am I going to do, I can't afford another one- how am I going to water the trees?" A minute later: "Well, my headache's gone away. And I'm not nauseous anymore either." Smiles. "You know, I think everything's going to work out."

Soula ends up buying another inverter, one

recommended to her by electrosensitive friends in Castle Valley, which has a smoother sine wave and less dirty electricity. She has our friend Chris build a concrete wall around it, which almost completely blocks the electrical field (the magnetic field does penetrate through, as almost nothing blocks a magnetic field, but this only extends out a few feet).

Homesteading

Sumi, big Mama of the goat herd, waddles into the milk shed, triple-D sized udder swinging pendulously back and forth like a shopaholic's purse after a big sale at Gucci. She steps up on the milking stanchion, pushes her head through the boards to the food tray, and begins chowing down (melon rinds, broccoli, cabbage leaves today, yum yums). I close her head in the restraints, wash her udder, grab the milk cup and start milking.

Milking a goat is like playing some weird musical instrument. You hold the teat up against the udder with your thumb and index finger (don't squeeze here), while rhythmically moving your other three fingers down the teat to form a ball of milk and then squeeze it out into the cup. The milk in the cup foams up and is perfect for adding to coffee. Today I'm having chaga-mocha-mint with honey from the beehives, with Sumi milk on top; fifteen dollars at the cafes in New York City, I'm sure.

Sumi behaves, as long as the food tray stays full, but the other goat, Daisy, is a piece of work. She's an Alpine goat, brown with black markings, scrawny, and foaming at the mouth like she's rabid (an aftereffect of eating apricot pits, which are poisonous to goats). Daisy loves to wipe this foamy drool all over the food tray, me, and the other goats, whatever is convenient. Sumi reminds me of an African queen, proud and regal...but if Daisy was a human, she'd be a trailer park lady with curlers in her hair, who chain smokes Marlboros and throws dishes across the yard at her neighbors.

Daisy's the hardest goat to milk, because her udder is hard and the orifices of the teats are too small, so the milk comes out in tiny squirts and takes forever to finish. It hurts my hand and I'm concerned about getting carpal tunnel. If that's not bad enough, she stomps her feet, throws the food on the floor and tips over the tray, and of course slobbers all over everything, all the while looking at me sideways with love in her eyes. There's nothing like a goat to teach you patience.

Sumi and Daisy hate each other. This started the moment they met each other, when Daisy took one look at Sumi and immediately butted her in the udder. Sumi responded by butting her back, and it's been like that ever since. Sumi, due to her size, is the dominant one, but Daisy will sneak up on her and butt her in the udder, or will walk over to Sumi's hay and poop on it. What Soula didn't realize when she bought them, from two different farms in Castle Valley, is that goats are racist. Sumi is a Nubian and Daisy is an Alpine (To further complicate the matter, the "teenage" girls, Star and Patches, are mixed breed, with Sumi's son as the father and Daisy as the mother. So there's always all this drama).

Even when goats hate each other, they still seek out each others' company, and Sumi and Daisy are often seen just chilling together on opposite sides of the fence in their separate pens. They are "frenemies." Goats, I'm learning, are emotionally complex creatures, as friendly as a cat or dog but with the urge to always be "contrary," and always on the lookout for something to get into. I learn to "read" the looks in their shifty sideways eyes, and to anticipate their next move before the goat even knows what it's going to do.

Milking the goats becomes my job, and it's what keeps me going through the months and years here at the farm. There's something calming about putting my head against a goat's flank and milking her. I'm in the zone, and I find that the goats respond to my energy and are calm if I'm calm (though Daisy causes trouble just for shits and giggles). On some afternoons we take the goats for walks around the property and into the canyon beyond. They eat saltbush, sage, dock, juniper, pine, pretty much everything really, and I watch them and watch clouds move across the sky and think, how much longer will we be safe out here? The end of the Earth, it feels like. For now.

Our town is a small ranching community where there's enough space between the neighbors that you can see the smoke from their fireplace but you can't pick up a signal from their Wi-Fi. There's a small charter school/library, a store that isn't open, a post office, a couple churches, some houses. One 3G phone tower (later changed to 4G, but blocked completely by the hill at the farm), a couple smaller antennas on a nearby ranch (also out of range at Soula's). A couple stop signs. No traffic lights.

It's the kind of place where kochia and tumbleweed line the roadsides and people will give you the two-fingered wave from their car or pickup as you pass each other. A place where people mind their business but if you need help you know who to call. The kind of place where no one looks at you that strangely if you've got a goat riding in the passenger seat of your car (but all that comes later). At night you can look out across the valley at the city lights (all two of them) while a billion stars twinkle overhead and the dogs and coyotes hurl insults at each other across the sagebrush.

My first couple years at the farm, I stay in isolation in our little bubble. I lose touch with everyone except Soula, Jess and our friend Chris (and various others, who come and go like characters in a soap opera). I milk goats, make cheese, take care of 70 chickens, shovel goat pens, plant gardens, cook, pick fruit, dry and can fruit, work with beehives, make compost, joke around with Soula as I'm doing the dishes in the morning. Work is life. Work has meaning. Sometimes I feel like shit. But keep going. Focus. Milk the goats.

Occasionally I have to go out into the world, if I have to get a tooth pulled or something equally serious. Out in the world I'm dizzy, dazed from electricity, and my sense of where all these little towns are is vague, like towns in a n storybook. I ride in the back of Soula's car, leather jacket zipped tight against the signal, bag of herbal inflammation remedies close at hand. It's serious shit going out there. Go, accomplish your mission, get back to the farm. A day or two recovery time is usual, with headaches and nausea, though of course I still have to milk goats and feed chickens. It helps. Stay in my routine. Don't think too hard. Eat good food, make jokes, work.

Soula does everything 100% organic on her farm: no pesticide-sprayed food, no disgusting cleaning chemicals, only natural-fibered clothing. Chemical and gluten-sensitive herself, she is an amazing cook and the things she teaches me about diet are what helps me to finally regain my health.

Enzymes are key, Soula says: lots of fruit, salads, avocados, raw dairy, and never have any cooked oils (this includes frying, stir-frying, cooked eggs or fatty meat), because this is what clogs up your gallbladder and arteries. Raw fats are fine, such as olive oil on top of food after it's done cooking, but if you cook the oils it changes them and makes it harder for the liver to process so the waste may just build up in your body if your digestive system has been compromised in any way.

"Think about it this way," says Soula when explaining this concept. "It's like putting used oil into an engine. It just won't work as well."

Neither Soula or I miss pizza or fried foods or grande super nachos, because when you eat simple, whole food that comes from the earth, your taste buds detoxify and you can actually taste the flavors in your food. We share many meals over the years on the farm, from millet pancakes to "R'apple pie (raw apple pie) to vegetable soups and wild mushroom-flavored quinoa. We also enjoy fruit from her orchard: mulberries, cherries, apricots, apples, plums, peaches, pears, and wild foods too such as banana yucca fruits.

I go through a couple years of bad health until my gallbladder sludge finally clears out from the good diet, and I cure the Candida infection with an enzyme supplement called Candex.

Now I feel great and can haul water buckets and shovel the goat pens all I want, and go for barefoot runs up the canyon. But I'm still electrosensitive. The world outside is still out of the question. I'm 38. Am I going to be on this farm my whole life? It's okay…but it doesn't feel like enough. I need my own space to shine and contribute my gifts to the world. If only I could get my own land.

"Well, why can't you?" Says Soula. "You know, I got this land as a single mother on Disability. I didn't have any more money than you do now. I just made up my mind I could do it- and sometimes I couldn't afford shoes for Jess when he was a kid, he probably still resents me for it- but I just worked as hard as I could and now look what I have."

"I'd have to tie a lot of sage bundles to afford land," I say. "I can't get a real job and it's out of the question for me to get Disability for electrosensitivity…"

"You just have to put your intention to it," she says. "Don't think about what you can't do, or worry about how it's going to happen. Just focus and pray, and you'd be amazed what can happen."

Sure, I think. But I decide to do it anyway, to focus on the fact that I need to have property. I could start my own community, a research facility to study creative solutions for living with electrosensitivity. There aren't any other options, so this has to happen.

An Unexpected Turn of Events

In 2020 the whole world goes crazy. Absolutely nothing here changes at all, except that the skies are cleaner now that there's no airplanes flying. At first we're thinking that "the shit has hit the fan" and society is finally going to collapse (Or has it collapsed already, I ask Soula, maybe you should turn on the Internet and check). We've got a basement full of canned fruit, sacks of grain, and of course the goats and gardens. We order a few more sacks of millet and quinoa from Moonflower. I make sure to get extra coffee.

Soula tells stories of how Moab looks like a ghost town with empty streets. The mask comes in handy for blocking gross chemical smells, she says, and the six-foot social distancing is great for staying away from peoples' cell phones. We read online that people are getting psychological problems from isolation, and I think, fuck you normies, with your Netflix and Amazon delivery and ice cold drinks whenever you want them, your whole family together in the quarantine. You have no idea (That said: I do actually have compassion for people, especially kids, because I understand the long-term psychological damage that can result from isolation).

A friend tells me that you can get special pandemic Unemployment by applying on the Unemployment website and choosing Self-employed. Sounds too good to be true, I say. No, my friend assures me, it works. Well, I am a house painter by trade. And I do happen to be unemployed at this time. And there is this pandemic that would prevent me from getting work. I go on the website and fill out some forms, and holy shit, it works. Within a few months I've saved up thousands of dollars. Well, what am I going to do with it?

One hot July day when we're coming back from a trip up to the mountains- we like to go up here in the summer to swim at the waterfall and look for new plants- Soula decides on a whim to swing by a property that's for sale. A bumpy driveway leads through sagebrush and juniper desert to a cleared area, where there's a 70's style trailer with a tin roof next to it, a well, and a shed. All the amenities I'd really need to get started.

But it's the view that's amazing: towering sandstone cliffs behind the property (bordered by public lands), and in the front you can look out across the valley and see farm fields with grazing cows, cottonwoods, more red cliffs across the valley. Not a cell tower in sight. Very few neighbors. Close to the road but hidden (but I can see whoever's coming). Close to the river. I just have this feeling that I'm supposed to be here. So I put my powers of intention on overdrive: please God, help me to live here.

I call the realtor. I put my nervousness aside and just fake confidence, acting like I know what I'm doing. I tell her I'm interested, and we begin corresponding. The property is listed at $55,000. Soula urges me to offer $40,000. Seems too ballsy, I think. Maybe she'll say no. But I put in an offer anyway. The landowner says yes!

Now, there's the little problem of that I only have $10,000. Can I get a bank loan? I call my bank, and, same thing, I fake confidence. They do a credit check, and they say no, but maybe I can get someone to cosign. My parents say they'll think about it.

Meanwhile, negotiations with the realtor continue. I continue bluffing, and don't let her know I have no money. Several days of anxiety and hope. I forget to add the rennet to coagulate the milk into cheese at least once. Soula says, focus, girl, Earth to Julia, and we laugh. And then, after they'd given it much thought, my parents call to tell me they've decided to give me the rest of what I need to buy the land. A gift. I don't even owe them back. Holy shit. What did I do to deserve this?

I think it was my time in Vermont that did it. They realized my struggles were for real, and they wanted to help me. Well, they definitely get a lifetime supply of free goat cheese.

2021

2021 is a year of work, the hardest I've ever worked: all the logistical things that have to be done before I can move onto my property. Land surveys, calls to the county, hiring a well digger to replace the well's broken AC pump with a DC pump, hiring Chris to hook up a bunch of old solar panels to power the well, cleaning trash off my property, apprenticing with Chris to learn basic carpentry skills (we build a cabin at Soula's farm), building a goat barn and corral on my land with Chris, drywalling and painting Chris' house in town to pay him back for his help (getting zapped by the Smartmeter the whole time and feeling terrible), and meanwhile, in my spare time, milking four goats, making cheese, doing dishes, taking care of 70 chickens, filling water buckets for all the animals, and tying sage bundles and packaging eggs to make a little extra cash.

2021 is a hot year, a drought year, and smoke from wildfires stifles the valley in a dead haze. It's sometimes hard to make myself get up and face another day, but the promise of my land is what keeps me going. Finally, in August, everything is ready, and I move across the valley to my property with two milk goats.

Living in a trailer, filling water buckets from the tap, drinking goat milk lattes in the morning and looking out across the valley at this landscape of red cliffs and juniper trees: some people might call this roughing it. But I feel like I've won the game.

(Photo credit: Soula Marie)

Electrosafe Building Solutions

Metal Shielding vs. Bio-Absorbent Shielding

Do a quick Google search for electromagnetic shielding, and what you'll come up with is a long list of vendors advertising various types of metal mesh- embedded materials. The idea is that the metal, being electrically conductive, conducts the electricity down into the ground, thus protecting whatever is behind it, the way a Faraday cage works. Copper and silver, being highly electrically conductive, are the most common metals are the most commonly used metals, but other metals such as aluminum are also used. All of this stuff is expensive, which is discouraging for electrosensitives who just want a safe place to sleep and not be in pain.

According to Gary, who has thirty plus years of actual En Terra (on the ground) research and experience finding EMF solutions that actually work (and for him it is a life and death situation, not just theory), Faraday cages are "Bullshit."

The way he explained it to me, as we sat one day on a sandstone rock overlooking miles of red rock desert and junipers in a remote part of the Utah desert, is that, "When electricity hits metal and interacts with it, the metal changes the electricity and creates an electromagnetic field, and re-radiates it outward. And electrosensitives will almost always begin to react to these changed frequencies."

"So it doesn't work?"

"Let me put it this way. One time I put up a wall of galvanized copper mesh- spent a fortune on it- and after awhile I began to realize there was a new field at the site, inflammation in the meridian points...drove myself crazy trying to figure it out, and I finally realized it was coming from the wall. I took down the copper and it went away."

"So what does work?"

"Differentially Absorbent Electromagnetic Shielding Systems are the only thing that works."

What are Differentially Absorbent Electromagnetic Shielding Systems? Basically, anything natural: rocks, sand, wood, natural fibers, cardboard (which is made from wood fibers). Also, some synthetic materials, such as fiberglass window screen. The idea is that these materials absorb wireless radiation, so your body's tissues don't have to.

Gary showed me a wall he'd made out of a big piece of plywood, painted with a mixture of sand and wood glue that he calls "Carleenite," and he had me put on the headphones and listen to the signal coming through his Acoustimeter. In front of the plywood wall, in line with the mountains where there was a cell tower, I could hear a faint, but unpleasant, disgusting-sounding signal, kind of like feedback on a microphone. Behind the wall, the signal was quieter, more staticky.

"Every natural material has a different part of the electromagnetic spectrum that it absorbs," said Gary, "And a different rate of attenuation."

"Attenuation?"

"Think about it this way," he said, drawing a curved sine wave in the sand with a stick. "This is the carrier wave. And this," he said, scribbling a jagged, choppy line over the first wave, "Is the pulsed modulation. Now these materials don't block the signal completely, but what they do is to cause a gradual loss of flux intensity through the medium, taking off some of the jagged edges."

"Like it's sanding the edges down?"

"Exactly. Now since each of the natural materials has a different part of the spectrum that it absorbs and attenuates, the way we do it is we use layers of different materials- cardboard, stone, wood, Carleenite, foam insulation, basically the criteria is that it's free, it's cheap, or it comes from the Dumpster and we're keeping it out of the landfill."

"I like that," I said, thinking about the expense and complication of making Faraday cages.

"I like to use at least four materials," he said, "Four is the magic number in building. Four or twelve. We layer all these materials and, even if we don't know exactly which parts of the spectrum each material attenuates, it's likely to work. And you can test it with your meter."

Gary says I have a great mind for understanding this stuff, which surprises me, because no one had ever told me that before. But of course, at my jobs in the past, my mental facilities had most likely been compromised by electromagnetic fields without my even knowing it. I just thought I was stupid. Now, the longer I live away from the fields, the smarter I get, and more importantly, my neuroplasticity increases, my ability to learn new skills.

Not only that, but I actually enjoy building stuff, now that it's within my grasp. The first thing I built by myself was a three-sided outhouse hole screen, made of pallets nailed together (this was before I bought the screw gun). It looked pretty bad. After that, I built a four-sided, double-stacked pallet shower (I ran a garden hose through the slats). It looked even worse. But my third completed project, a roof to cover my hay bales, actually looks good, and the hay bales are still dry.

One of the many problems in my life as an electrosensitive refugee was lack of shelter. I was always looking for a good cave, but more often than not there wasn't one. The non-Wi-Fi'd zones of the world are cold, hot, buggy, windy…basically the places where civilized people don't want to be. I suffered a lot. Often there were things lying around like pallets, scrap wood, and nails. If I'd known then what I know now, I could have had a much better life.

I had this misconception that building was this complicated thing that was out of my reach. I thought you had to be strong, mechanically inclined, or a guy, to be able to figure it out. This is not true. Certainly, carpentry is a skilled profession that can take a lifetime to master, but, just as anyone can learn to put dandelions in a salad without going to herbalism school, anyone who wants to can learn how to screw together a few pallets and make a dry place to sleep.

You don't need a palace. You just need a place to sleep where there isn't dirty electricity coming out of the outlets and a Wi-Fi router zapping you from the next room. Small is good. Learn a few basic skills and you can put up a shelter in whatever safe place you've found, even if it is just a corner of the backyard. Once you have walls and a roof, there are other things you can do to help protect you from outside EMF.

Basic tools to acquire include a screw-gun (hex-head screws are best, and also get a roofing bit and roofing screws), power saw, hammer, level, tape measure, and shovel. Battery-powered tools are safer than corded tools for electrosensitives (though not completely safe, because remember that anything with a motor puts off an AC field).

Here is a list of materials to consider in your low-tech, low-cost, EMF-safe shelter-building endeavors.

Pallets

Pallets are great for off-grid living. Out here in the country, we use them to build everything: sheds, chicken coops, outhouses, fences, whatever. They are free at many places in town. You can load a bunch of them into a truck and just screw them together for walls. Great addition to my Post-Apocalyptic Stone Age decor.

Plywood

I put plywood up over the pallets to finish the wall. Often, I can't afford whole sheets, so I just piece together whatever scraps of plywood and other random pieces of scrap lumber I can find. My goat sheds, shower, and outhouse are done this way. Oh no, what will the neighbors think? Oh wait, the neighbors are just as crazy as me, it doesn't matter.

By the way, make sure you're using real plywood and not particle board. Particle board, while it does help block EMF, is toxic and will dissolve if rained on, and the goats will eat it and get sick.

Rocks

Rocks are a common sight in the desert where I live. They are sturdy, free, and best of all, they block EMF. So it makes sense to use them in your building: for walls, floors, or foundations for pallet structures. The downside of rocks is that they are heavy. My plan is to wait until the boy goats get bigger, and then put those good for nothing freeloaders to work hauling rocks for me.

Cedar Posts

I cut down dead, straight juniper trees to make into fence posts. When you've got your post ready, dig a one and a half foot hole with a post hole digger or a shovel. Put a handful of gravel in first, then insert the post, then add some Quikcrete (ready-mixed concrete), then add some water, mix with a stick or a trowel (I use a metal tamping tool), and do a few layers of this until the hole is filled, tamping it down as you go. You can mix a few stones in with the concrete for added strength.

You can put these in without the concrete, if you add layers of small rocks and crush it down with a tamping tool on each layer. "It's what all the old cowboys did, you don't need concrete," my neighbor says. Others say it's better to use concrete. I've done some of both, so I'll just see which lasts longer, if I can remember which is which.

These cedar posts work well as fence posts, or as corner posts on a building or roof.

Roofs

Metal, as discussed previously, is problematic for many electrosensitives because it can enhance an electromagnetic field. That said, not all electrosensitives appear to react to metal (I've been sleeping in aluminum campers for years and don't notice any adverse effects), and its usefulness in building may outweigh the risks. This should be determined on a case to case basis, and I think it also depends on what you are building and its proximity to you.

I use metal roofs for goat pens and hay sheds. I put it up over a framework of 2X6's and 2X4's, screwed down with roofing screws. The sheets are fairly easy to work with, and I have had three people so far donate metal roofing to me, mostly left over pieces from previous projects. So, I have a three-colored roof, but it works.

For a sleep structure, in which it is important to have the environment as field-free as possible, I plan on using non-metallic types of materials, covered in dirt.

Gates and Doors

Pallets make great doors. So do old doors, which often can be found for free or cheap. You can buy new hinges from the hardware store, or find them cheap at thrift stores, or scavenge them from broken doors in trash piles. Use the screw gun to attach them.

Sandbag/Earthbag

Definitely great for blocking EMF, and low budget. You buy the bags, and put them into a special holder while you fill them with sand, then stack them to whatever shape you want, putting scrap barbed wire between each layer of bags. Then you cover the top in a stucco made of clay/sand and straw.

I have played with this a little in the past but have not done any on my property. I do know that Earth bag building is labor-intensive, useless for insulation, and the bags degrade over time, and you're always having to re-patch the walls. So it might not be something I'll personally do, but some people like it.

Insulation

Cardboard boxes are great for insulation! They are also great for EMF- blocking. Break them down, take off tape or labels (a paring knife or jackknife works well for these steps), and stuff them in between the slats of the pallets, as many as you can fit. Then put the plywood over the top of the whole thing when you are done. Soula swears by this, because she once insulated an entire cabin with cardboard and found that after she was done, the bars on a cell phone dropped to one bar where it had previously showed five bars.

Gary is also a fan of the pink foam board insulation because it blocks EMF. As long as it is older and is not still off gassing, it should be relatively safe to use, especially if it is enclosed in between the plywood layers, but do make sure it's not going to crumble into the environment. You also have to make sure it doesn't get wet, because black mold can give you EHS.

Carleanite

Named after Gary's daughter Carly, Carleanite is an EMF-blocking substance developed by Gary, made from sand and wood glue. It works remarkably well. Here is the recipe.

1 .Sift sand through a scrap of window screen into a container.

2 .Mix Titebond III glue (must use III) half and half with water. A yogurt container works well for this purpose.

3. Pour the glue into the sand, slowly, and mix with a pallet knife until it is the consistency of thick mud.

4. Prime surfaces first with just the water/Titebond mixture.

5. Paint with the sand/Titebond (Carleanite) using a paintbrush.

6. Do multiple layers (dry in between layers).

Variations: Fiberglass window screen also has EMF-blocking properties. Gary will sometimes use this in between layers of Carleanite. Another thing I've done is to substitute shungite powder for the sand, and use this as one layer between layers of the Carleanite. Soula has mixed shungite with clay paint (Bioshield is a good non-toxic brand), and reports that it helps significantly.

Living with Electricity (as Safely as Possible) How to Hardwire Internet

Take a look at your modem, and first determine if it is a modem/router combination (most are these days). If it is, disable the Wi-Fi. Sometimes there is a switch, sometimes not. If not, you can Google the modem name + disable Wi-Fi for instructions on how to do this. If you still can't figure this out, it is possible to just buy a new modem, one that either doesn't have Wi-Fi or has an easy switch.

Go around your house and decide where you'll want the Internet ports to be.

Get an Ethernet switch, and plug it into your modem with Cat 6 cable. Run Cat 6 Cable to all the ports in the house where you'll want to plug in a computer. You can use horseshoe nails or screws to attach the cable to the wall, or bury it outside if it is running between buildings.

How to Set up a Landline

Call the phone company and have them set one up. They may try to talk you out of it, and many areas are phasing out landlines. Insist on it. Also don't be afraid to tell them why you need a landline. They need to know, and many telecommunications workers are noticing adverse health effects themselves since 5G was installed, so you may be helping someone out.

Get an old style phone with a cord, and put it somewhere

comfortable where you spend a lot of time. Make sure to not get a cordless phone, as they are much worse than cell phones. Also, as cool as those retro phones with the dials are, don't get one, because they don't work for entering in numbers when you get a business's message board (my parents have one, I know).

To complicate things, some electrosensitives also react to landlines, because the Internet and phone signals come in on the same line. To solve this, Soula had the phone company come out and split the Internet and phone into two lines. She now has two bills, but says it is worth it because we don't get headaches from the phone anymore.

Household AC Power

If you already have a house that is wired for AC, there are things you can do to minimize exposure. Locate the switchboard in your house, and turn off everything you aren't using. In Soula's house, which is a small, one-person house, she just turns off the master switch at the top whenever we aren't using the power. We turn on the wall to charge computers, for example, or we'll turn on the hot water to do dishes. She runs the fridge at night or when we are out walking the goats. This situation works for Soula, who reacts less to AC household power than I do.

I use a "pole flipper," my invention: a ten-foot pole with a horseshoe nail at the end, with which I can stand safely back to flip the switches on and off. The pole flipper is also useful for retrieving things I may have left in the electric zone (my hat for example), and also works for opening the front door for cats.

Sometimes I housesit for Soula when she goes on trips, and during those times I keep the power off, except for when using the Internet and charging the computer. I keep food in a cooler on the back porch in the winter. For lights at night, I use a headlamp with rechargeable batteries. I charge the batteries when I charge my computer. Usually I choose this time to walk my goats.

Off-Grid Solar

The main components of a simple off-grid electrical system are the solar panels, the charge controller, the batteries, and the inverter. The solar panels harvest energy, the batteries store it, the inverter converts DC to AC power (if you need it), and the charge controller mediates between all these components.

For my system on my land, I was able to acquire most of the parts secondhand. The exception was the inverter, which was about $200 on Amazon (and, at 2,000 watts, is probably more than I need and a smaller one might also be safer). The inverter is the only part of this system that is not safe for electrosensitives, but AC power is necessary to charge my laptop, power tool batteries, flashlight batteries, and battery-powered blender. I only turn the inverter on when I'm charging batteries, and I use a pole flipper, standing back to flip the switch on after I've plugged in my devices, and coming back to turn it off in this same way after a couple hours.

If I wanted to, I could run DC power such as lights or a DC mini-fridge directly from the system's batteries. Or I could use the inverter and a power cord to run a vacuum cleaner, corded power saw, or AC mini-fridge (but the AC uses would bother me, so I mostly don't do this).

My well is on a separate solar array. It has a DC pump (a Grundfos, is you're ever looking for one: pricey, but it's the only DC well pump that is worth getting). Currently I have running water only when the sun is shining, but it would be a simple thing to hook it up to batteries so I can have running water anytime.

There is information online about how to set up your own DIY system, but unless you enjoy this type of challenge it may be worth it to do what I did, which is hire someone to hook it up.

Third World Magic Fridge

Also called a Zeer pot. This really works. You get a big terra cotta pot (five gallons if you can find one), nest a smaller terra cotta pot inside it (such as a three-gallon), and then fill the space between the pots with sand. It is best if the pots' rims are at the same level when they are nested. Cover the inner pot with a terra cotta lid (the saucers that are sold with the pots work for this). Then cover the whole top with a wet rag.

Store food in the inner pot, and keep the rags and sand wet. I usually have to add water twice on average during the hot months. You actually want to keep this in a sunny place, as it works by evaporate cooling. It can keep a bottle of milk as cold as if it was in a refrigerator. It doesn't work as well for things like meat or cheese that don't benefit from a moist environment, but unopened packages of meat and cheese are just fine.

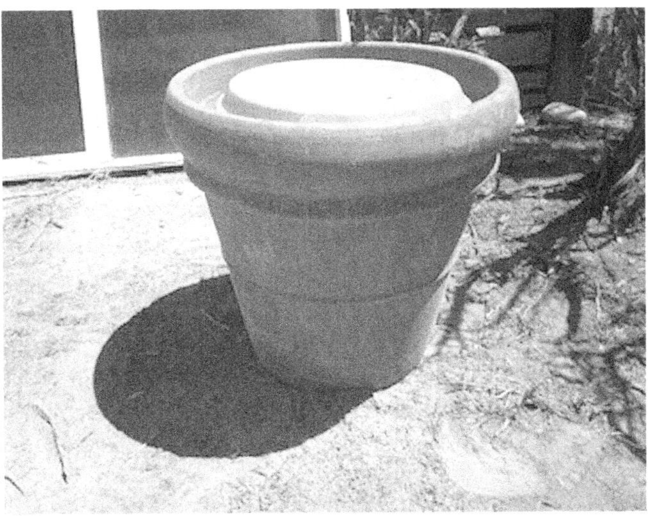

Clothing and Bedding

As I said before, I'm not a fan of silver-embedded EMF-protective clothing myself (although some electrosensitives swear by it, and there may be a place for it in the wardrobe, especially for acute situations where you have to be exposed to high frequency RF for a short period of time). What I am a fan of is natural clothing that has a negative electrostatic charge. Natural materials, which include cotton, wool, leather, linen, and rayon, have a negative electrostatic charge, which is good for the body and may enhance your resistance against harmful EMF. Some of these, especially leather and wool, also block out some of the EMF, and "attenuate" it (smooth out the jagged peaks and valleys of the waveform so it is less harmful).

Polyester clothing (and blends) is made of plastic and tends to build up a positive electrostatic charge, which is just one more thing that overloads the body's meridian system and brings you that much closer to having an EMF reaction. They also can catch on fire easily, and melt against your skin, which happened to Soula's brother years ago and gave him third-degree burns all over his body. Natural fiber clothing doesn't do this. To avoid spontaneous human combustion while cooking over a campfire, be sure to wear natural fiber clothing.

Multiple layers of different materials is best for protection, says Gary, the same as with building. I sometimes wear a wool hat over a leather hat in winter. Or a wool sweater over cotton shirts. And I never go to town without my leather coat. It's a great excuse to look cool. Soula swears by leather, and says it's been one of the things that has helped her the most in her travels. She'll also put a leather coat over peoples' Wi-Fi routers if she's visiting someone and they won't turn it off, and says it helps.

I recently was gifted a super cool leather aviator helmet by a local artist. I wear it now whenever I go out in the car, and I feel that it helps.

If you're into jewelry, having metal on your body as an electrosensitive is generally a bad idea. When I found out I was electrosensitive, I replaced my metal glasses frames with plastic and stopped wearing any necklaces or rings with metal in them. I don't usually react to metals, but no point in taking any chances. One time recently, I decided to try on a copper-wrapped crystal pendant of mine, and after typing for awhile on my computer I realized I had a slight burning sensation in my hands and forearms. I took the pendant off, and the feeling went away. It will make a nice window decoration.

Rocks and crystals wrapped in twine are a better option for jewelry. They might not save you from EMF, but they can't hurt, and they're pretty. I wear shungite bracelets and am happy with them. It may be that they put off a negative charge like the natural clothing does.

As far as shoes go, rubber is an insulator and, on your feet, prevents the body from dumping excess positive charge into the ground. It is hard to find shoes that don't have rubber soles, but you should find some if you can.

I've heard that the best material to have as bed sheets is linen, and that it will help ground you and will never build up a positive charge. I haven't tried this yet as I get most of my stuff at thrift stores, but I do use cotton sheets and wool or cotton blankets. For camping and wintertime, I still use polyester sleeping bags because I haven't been able to come up with a lightweight, warm solution.

While we're on the topic of wearables, I have been doing some experiments with magnets. I researched into Magnetic Pair Therapy, which places a pair of strong neodymium magnets- one with the positive side facing your skin, the other with the negative- on specific point pairs on the body. Proponents of this therapy claim that it helps treat various ailments such as pain and inflammation, and that it helps the body to heal itself.

I decided to try a variation of this therapy, by placing the magnets on a pair of acupuncture points recommended to me by an acupuncturist friend (in my case they were SJ 5 and GB 41, but different ones may be more relevant for different people). Although Magnetic Pair Therapy recommends using a positive and a negative, I personally felt nothing but negative effects from positive magnets, and positive effects from negative magnets. So, I modified it by only using the magnets facing negative side against my skin.

It seems that when I use the negative magnetism during or after an EMF exposure, it helps my body to recharge and ground itself quicker. I've tried them on these points (which are on my wrist, so I made bracelets by taping them to the underside of a leather band, and on my feet so I taped them to sandals). I also made a headband with one sewed into it, so I could put it against the spot of my head that hurts around Wi-Fi. I've also tried taping them to the sides of my glasses so they rest against my temples.

What I've found in myself is that these magnets have subtle effects that seem beneficial to me. More experimentation is needed. Also be advised that as this is a new technology for EHS and is unstudied and everyone's body is different, it is possible that you could actually do some harm, especially with the positive poles of the magnets. Don't use them when you are actually touching an electronic device such as a computer, as it could mess up the computer and possibly cause the fields from the computer to induct into your body in unknown ways.

Pack Goats

"Come on Andy, good boy!" I shout as Andy, my long-legged, black and white lead goat gallops toward me, ears flapping. "Good Stanley! Good Tito!" The others come running too, barrel-chested, long-horned Stanley, and calm, fluffy Tito. I'm training these little fellows to be pack goats. They're still kids now, but at four years old they'll be able to wear pack saddles and carry fifty pounds of gear each on trips into the backcountry. As the rest of the world moves into a nightmare of self-driving, 5G'd cyber shit, here in Bedrock I'm looking into the past for my transportation options (and mine are a lot cuter, though Musk says his cyber vehicles will also make goat noises; if you don't believe me, look it up).

I let the boys chow down on a saltbush for awhile. All goats are obnoxious little shits by nature, and most of training is about showing them who's boss. Pain is not a motivator to any creature that head butts each other for fun, but if you can outwit them they will respect you and consider you "top goat." Squirt bottles work great. When the boys were little, I trained them to walk on leashes and to be tied to a fence. They also rode in the car with me when they were young, which was great for taming them. Actually, Andy still rides in the car with me. He pretty much fills up the passenger seat at this point, and he'll put his head in my lap the whole time and let me pet him. People do a double-take, at first thinking he's a dog, then noticing the horns.

I hope to go backpacking with them soon. Although the boys are still too small to carry much besides a few clothes, it will be fun.

I may take a milk goat with me too, so I can make yogurt in the backcountry. Between that, wild edibles, and whatever dried grains I carry, I could theoretically stay out there for months. It is my back up plan, if things ever get bad here (Musk's satellites may still be a problem, but I do know where there are some good caves).

5G Rollout

In the year 2020, when people were hiding in their houses distracted by Netflix, one of the "essential" jobs that did not go away was that of the telecom companies. Across the nation (and around the world), telecom workers lurked in suburban neighborhoods, surreptitiously installing small, rectangular antennas on schools, churches, public buildings, along highways, and on 3G and 4G towers. Now, these little white rectangles are everywhere, as ubiquitous and overlooked in the urban landscape as pigeons or empty McDonalds bags. Maybe I'm imagining things, but it seems that people in the cities and towns are getting sicker and crazier all the time. Out here in the boonies, nothing has changed.

5G, which stands for fifth generation (after 2G, 3G, and 4G), is a range of frequencies spanning the entire microwave spectrum (the various carriers own different parts of the spectrum, which they bid for when the FCC auctioned the frequencies off). While the previous "G's" only contained a few frequencies (900 and 1800 MHz for 2G, for example), 5G can include most of them (though not all are being implemented at this time).

5G is divided into low-band (300MHz to 3 GHz) , mid-band (3 GHz to 30 GHz), and high-band(30 GHz to 300 GHz). How it works is that the shorter waves deliver more data but only travel short distances and are easily blocked, and the longer waves travel farther and penetrate more (into buildings, trees, humans, etc.). The longer waves can be used as carrier waves for the shorter waves (but how well this is working right now is unknown; people are not reporting better phone reception). The high band are more biologically active, and are right below infrared and visible light on the spectrum chart. Most devices now run on 4G frequencies that are similar to the low-band 5G.

The high band are what is known as millimeter waves because they are about a millimeter long, and they are the type of radiation that airport body scanners use. It's "like living inside an airport body scanner at all times," said one researcher. It absorbs into human tissue skin-deep, at levels just below what would burn the skin. The "good news" is that the high-band 5G does not travel very far and, being "skin deep," can be easily blocked. Wearing leather clothing seems to protect against its effects significantly. Trees also block it, and telecom workers cut down the trees and bushes when they install a 5G antenna, although one theory is that this is actually because 5G kills the trees, and then people would notice this and ask too many questions. Pay attention: are there trees near the 5G antennas in your town. If so, are they alive? If only part of it is alive, is it the part closer to the antenna or farther?

The bad news is that 5G antennas are fucking everywhere, and are just one more thing that makes town hard to tolerate. The real purpose for these antennas (besides making people sick) is that they are the infrastructure for the Internet of Things and the self-driving cars. In "the future," all our stuff will have antennas in it to allow it to communicate with the Internet. This will allow data to be collected so that companies will know more about us and be better able to target us with ads. It will also allow the AI to predict our behavior, which could have all kinds of benefits for a surveillance-state government (not to sound paranoid, but...). Is this the kind of future you want to live in?

The electrosensitive community had been dreading the onset of 5G for years before it was first rolled out in 2020. Not much time left, I'd kept thinking. I'd assumed that the world would become completely uninhabitable overnight and that it would probably kill me, so I had to come to terms with that (not too hard, as I've been living on borrowed time ever since my 36th birthday in the cave).

Well, 5G has been rolled out worldwide now. The towers feel horrible when I'm near them. I avoid town even more, and only go when I absolutely have to go. Out here, I'm healthy and have lots of energy, better than I've been in years. After town, I'm shaky and have a headache, and my tolerance for annoying goat noises drops to almost zero. It is obvious to me that the general population in urban areas is experiencing devastating effects (similar to what we the electrosensitives experienced with 3G and 4G, and the onset of Smartmeters around 2011). All of the mental health issues, anxiety, fear, anger, heart attacks, blood clots, diabetes soaring through the roof, healthy people suddenly dropping dead for no apparent reason...from an observer's perspective on the outside, there does appear to be a direct correlation. I pity them, and for the first time I actually feel grateful that I became electrosensitive first. I had time to prepare.

There are a couple inspirational videos that I recommend if you need something to boost your morale; you can find them on YouTube, One is a video of a flock of cockatoos in Australia destroying a 5G tower. Another is a video of a telecom worker in Britain, who, after getting sick from installing 5G towers, borrowed a tank and used it to knock down 5G towers and set them on fire. He's in jail now, but continues to speak out against the dangers of 5G.

Know Your Enemy: What's up with Elon Musk?

I first started hearing about Elon Musk around 2018 when Chris, who's a huge fan of Elon Musk, would inform Soula and I every time SpaceX was about to launch another rocket, and then retreat into his camper for the rest of the day. Chris would also tell us how much money he had made or lost on his Tesla stocks each day, and how much closer he was getting toward being able to pay off his Cybertruck (I pictured some huge, Transformers-like beast that could swim, fly, and possibly even travel though time, and was not looking forward to its arrival as it almost certainly would have built in Wi-Fi).

Then I started hearing about Musk's plans to put up 5G satellites all over the Earth. Chris assured us that Elon was using a different type of shortwave radio signal that was not harmful. I was skeptical. Gary, of course said, "Bull Shit."

Who was this Musk character, anyway, and what exactly was his evil plan? I plugged in my landline computer, turned on the Internet switch with my ten-foot pole, and typed Elon Musk's name into Google to find out.

Elon Musk, whose companies are SpaceX, Tesla, Neuralink, The Boring Company, OpenAI, and most recently Twitter, is the richest person in the world. He was born in South Africa to wealthy parents. An entrepreneur from the start, Musk taught himself computer programming at age ten and sold his first computer game at age twelve. In the 90's, after moving to the United States as a young adult, Musk co-founded the web company Zip2 with his brother, and co- founded the online bank X.com, which later merged with another company to become PayPal. In the early 2000's Musk founded SpaceX and became CEO of Tesla, and later became interested in the fields of neurology and AI with his Neuralink and OpenAI companies. He gives large amounts of money to charity, is a proponent of free speech, and appears dedicated to helping humanity reach a utopian future where we all live happily ever after on Mars with our robot friends and communicate telepathically with Wi-Fi implants in our brains.

I listened to a few interviews with Elon Musk to get an idea of who he is. I have to say I was impressed with the way he speaks, which is personable with a matter-of-fact delivery of information that resonates with me. I admire his single- minded focus toward his goals, how he stays up at night obsessing over the details of the sensing system of his Tesla vehicles or whatever, until he gets it right. Musk says he "has little interest in material wealth" and that he's interested in his projects for their own sake. He sold all his houses and lives in a tiny house. He works alongside his employees at Tesla and often sleeps at the factory. As an obsessive nerd with single-minded focus on my own goals, I have respect for these qualities. Too bad he's not on our side. Too bad that my goals now include digging underground shelters with dirt roofs to protect myself from Musk's death rays in the sky.

On his Starlink satellites, Musk says: "It will be like having a cell tower in the sky," and says it will use the mid-band parts of the spectrum that cell phones already use, and will work with your current phone "to provide basic coverage to areas that are completely dead." T-Mobile is going to be giving this away for free with their most popular plans by the middle of 2023, and Elon is inviting other phone carriers to partner with him and also use his satellites. "No dead zones anywhere in the world for your cell phone," Elon says. "Big antennas on satellites, powerful antennas, and a lot of satellites."

Nowhere to run, nowhere to hide, I think. On the bright side, stranded hikers will now be able to call for help no matter where they are, which is good because, since EMF's interfere with sense of direction, there are going to be a lot more stranded hikers. Stranded bees and birds will be on their own.

Even scarier than Elon Musk's satellites is his work with Neuralink, which is an implant that you can put in your brain to be able to interface directly with AI and computers. It will be like "a Fitbit in your skull," Musk says. The Link will be connected through a simple surgery through micron-sized threads that will connect directly to neurons in the areas of the brain that produce movement. It will be first be used to treat conditions such as Alzheimer's, paralysis, and epilepsy, and later to give people "superpowers" such as enhanced memory, telepathy with other "Linked" people, and ability to surf the Web with your mind. This device has is already in use in animal trials (you can find a video of a monkey playing Pong on a computer with its mind). You will not be able to tell if a person has Neuralink just by looking at them, Elon says: "I could have a Neuralink right now and you wouldn't know it."

With Neuralink, people will be able to store and replay memories. They'll also be able to download programs to learn skills instantly, such as flying a helicopter, or learning to speak another language. "The way education works right now is it's extremely low bandwidth, extremely slow...lectures are the worst," says Elon. Call me old fashioned, but doesn't this defeat the whole purpose of being human? Isn't it better to build neural networks by actually learning things for yourself and having life experiences? Combine these "upgrades" with genetic modification of humans (which we've already seen in a small way, with mRNA vaccines), and we could be looking at the emergence of another species, Homo roboticus, which would outcompete the outdated, obsolete Homo sapiens who prefer to live a natural life and not be connected with the Borg.

Elon Musk says he is motivated by love of humanity: "I want to make sure there is a good future for humanity and that we're on a path toward understanding the meaning of the Universe, the meaning of life...why we are here and how did we get here." He also says, "I'm motivated more by curiosity that anything, and just to think about the future and not be sad."

Well, hearing Elon Musk talk makes me sad. As smart as Elon is, you'd think he'd be able to figure out that what he is doing could have catastrophic effects on all life on Earth. This leads me to believe that, either:

A. He is an Asperger's-type genius who only sees the engineering side of things and really does have peoples' best interests at heart.
B.

C. He does know, and doesn't care, because he has an agenda.
D. He's an AI himself.

I'd like to believe A, but what leads me toward B is that there is proof that Elon understands the link between biology and electricity: his explanations of Neuralink make this point clear. "Neurons communicate through electrical signals," Neuralink's website says. "We can record electrical signals in the brain." If Elon's really that smart, and if he cares about humanity, you'd think he would have looked into whether there was any possibility of his various inventions and devices interfering with biological life. But maybe he doesn't care, and would prefer to have a world populated by robots and cyborgs. Certainly the name of one of his newest kids, X Æ A-12, is rather suspicious.

I'm sure "X" and Elon will be safe from the onslaught of death rays that will be blasting the planet in the near future; they can just get an "upgrade" if anything goes wrong, and rewire their neurology to be "powered up" by the Wi-Fi instead of beaten down. Those of us who don't want anything to do with this bullshit had better start digging.

Birds and Electromagnetism

As a kid growing up in suburban Connecticut, and wishing I was somewhere like Montana or Colorado instead, birding for me was a link to that wilder world. I remember the downy woodpecker that I ID'd and then was "hooked" ever since. I remember the lark sparrow at Veteran's Park that I found through the Rare Bird Alert (which I called weekly on our landline, and knew the number by heart). Then there was the time I faked sick to stay home from school and saw my first yellow-rumped warblers. And the snow day when my best friend Daryl and I went sledding at the middle school and we saw a flock of cedar waxwings eating bittersweet berries in the bushes, and my brother was making fun of us but then admitted they were cool.

When I was 21 I got an internship working with the U.S. Fish & Wildlife Service's California Condor Recovery Program. The other interns and I monitored nests, took signals on the birds with radiotelemetry equipment, and put out dead cow carcasses for the condors to eat. Every week or so the condors (which are highly intelligent, and got bored now that they no longer had to search for their food) would decide to fly a couple hundred miles to ITT, which was the largest cell tower array in that part of California. They'd send one of us interns out there to chase the birds off the cell towers. I'd usually volunteer for the job, because I liked a good road trip.

ITT was a scrub oak and manzanita covered mountainside that would have been beautiful if it wasn't for the forest of giant Satan Trees at the top. We had our own key to the restricted area, and I'd let myself in and there would be the condors, perched on the towers like prehistoric beasts that went through a time warp. I'd come after them, waving my arms and yelling, they'd fly off, and I'd spend the rest of the day searching them out with my radio telemetry antenna and harassing them every time they landed. At night if the birds still hadn't gone home, I'd pull out my sleeping bag and settle down on the asphalt under the few stars and the blinking lights of the Satan Trees.

I never felt very good after a night at ITT (and often I would make a few wrong turns on the drive home). But never in a million years would I have made the connection. Two of the three condor nests failed that year.

Later, searching the Wildlife Job Board online, I noticed that many of the jobs involved counting dead birds at the base of cell towers. This sounded depressing, so I never applied for those jobs. I never thought too hard about *why* there were dead birds at the base of the cell towers.

I can look out my window now and see a few juncos poking around in the snow for seeds. I can hear a scrub jay, and if I look around I can probably find a white-crowned sparrow. If I drive out into the valley, I may see red-tailed hawks or bald eagles or kestrels out in the fields. At the pond, I might find a cinnamon teal. So there are birds…but, there should be more.

According to a recent episode of NPR's Science Friday, almost all North American bird families declined in number in recent years (the exception being ducks, which have increased in number). Alarmingly, the species that have declined the most are birds that have traditionally been the most adapted to humans, such as the chimney swift (cell phone antennas are often hidden on chimneys), and house sparrows (which live in cities). Hummingbirds, especially the rufous hummingbird (which migrates the farthest), and shorebirds and grassland birds (which also migrate long distances) were some of the hardest hit as well. The bobolink, a grassland bird that is strikingly patterned in black, white, and tan, and is one of the birds that migrates the farthest, is another bird that has massively declined.

NPR of course blamed climate change for the declines, and also mentioned pesticide use and habitat loss as possible factors, but they didn't say anything about cell towers. However, a previous episode of Science Friday had covered electromagnetism in birds, and they also have covered the electromagnetic sense in humans. They just refuse to connect the dots.

The day after I heard the NPR program, I happened to come across a short article about bobolinks in a 1984 issue of International Wildlife, which said that enough iron oxide (magnetite) had been found in the bird's heads to detect the Earth's magnetic field, and that it had been the first discovery of magnetic material in a migratory bird.

Since then there has been a lot more research into the magnetic navigational abilities of birds, and scientists have discovered tiny pieces of magnetite in many species of birds' brains which line up with the Earth's magnetic field (magnetite is also found in the brains and nervous systems of many other animals including humans). Birds also have specialized magnetic- sensing proteins in their eyes called cytochrome 4, which is thought to help them "see" magnetic fields. These discoveries explain how birds can migrate hundreds or thousands of miles every year and not get lost. Well, they used to not get lost, anyway.

These discoveries have personal significance to me. As a young person who learned to drive around the time cell phone towers were sprouting up everywhere, my sense of direction was legendarily bad. All those countless hours I spent lost in my gold '94 Saturn, driving around on some random backwoods road with no idea where I was, late for work and cursing my own stupidity...the jobs I lost, the appointments I missed, how stupid I felt at school when I would forget how to get to my classes, how stupid everyone else thought I was, all the booze I drank to swallow the pain...now I'm thinking, maybe it wasn't really my fault. Maybe my internal compass was spinning in circles.

I can take my binoculars now and go for a birdwatching hike and not get lost at all. In fact, my directional sense seems pretty good. I'm not sure how I should feel about all this. Should I be angry? Or should I laugh at the absurdity of life? And why not both?

Yellow-rumped (Audubon's) Warbler (Photo credit: Soula Marie)

Electrosensitivity in the Media

You know about product placement, where companies pay to have their product inserted into movies or TV shows, in order to embed it into the public's consciousness, in order to generate sales. Well, companies also pay to have ideas inserted into popular media, in order to influence culture. For example, if a telecommunication company wants the public to think a certain way about electrosensitives, it may pay the film studio to put certain messages into their programming.

One television show that has been popular in recent years is Better Call Saul. I'd heard that this show had an electrosensitive character, and that the show was pretty good, so I decided to check out a few clips of the show on YouTube. What I saw was that Chuck McGill, the protagonist Saul's brother, was a generally unlikeable, unsympathetic character who lived in isolation due to his electrosensitivity. Shrouded in tinfoil and living in a dark house, he only emerged, vampire-like, when he was up to no good. The details of Chuck's electrosensitivity were mostly all wrong, for example he is shown to be allergic to cell phones but also to the batteries from wristwatches (worn by other people, across the room), and to magnets. Also, he is shown to be "safe" in his house with the power all off, but the house is not shielded from outside EMF such as cell towers. This makes no sense. Over the course of the show, it is inferred that the EHS all in his head.

How might this portrayal of an electrosensitive influence the way the general public thinks about EHS? First off,

Chuck is kind of a villain, which is fine in itself, as bad people can be electrosensitive too, and not all of us are nice (to quote Gary: "Nice guys finish last."). However, since this is many peoples' first exposure to EHS, it immediately gives them a negative association. Worse, since Chuck's EHS is revealed to be psychosomatic, an uninformed person may then assume that real electrosensitives are psychosomatic too, without bothering to do their own research.

So, the result is they make us look crazy. And, I'll admit, that's not hard to do (says the lady who drives around with goats in her car, is digging an underground hideout, and turns the power on and off with a ten foot pole). Way to pick an easy target, you bullies.

The reality of the situation is that all the electrosensitives that I know are smart, courageous, heroic people who love nature, who look for creative solutions, and who must continually put ourselves into danger (town) on a regular basis and usually still manage to smile about it.

The Body Electric, or Reprogrammable Hardware?

I'm noticing shifting attitudes in the mainstream medical about bioelectricity, and I'm wondering what to make of it. Robert O. Becker, author of *The Body Electric* and *Cross Currents*, is famous in the electrosensitive community for his experiments in healing with DC electric currents in the 60's through the 80's. Robert O. Becker worked at the Veteran's Administration Hospital in Syracuse as the chief of orthopedics, and was a professor at SUNY. In his spare time he did experiments with electricity.

In his lab, Becker took Planaria, which are aquatic flatworms with a primitive brain and nervous system that have the ability to regenerate new heads or tails when you cut them into pieces. He was able to measure DC currents in the Planaria's body at the site of injury, and by reversing the current was able to grow a head where the tail should be and vice versa.

Becker next took salamanders, which are able to regenerate limbs, and measured DC voltages at the site of an amputated limb, and noted that the voltage changed from its normal -10mV to +20mV and then -30mV, until the limb was finished regrowing, at which point it would reset to its normal -10mV. He then amputated frogs' limbs, and noted that the voltage changed from -10mV to +20mV when the limb was amputated, and it would heal over but not regrow, and then revert back to -10mV. Then, Becker took electrodes and applied the salamander's levels of voltage to the amputation site on frog limbs, and the limbs grew back. He then began experimenting with rats and was getting some promising results. He then began to apply these principles with his osteopathy patients, and was able to achieve some bone healing with the application of silver electrodes (though nothing so extreme as a leg growing back).

Mainstream medical was not thrilled about Becker's work at the time, especially when he began to speak out about the dangers of manmade EMF. He protested a proposed high voltage power line in New York State, presented his testimony in court of electricity's biological effects, and soon after lost his funding from SUNY and lost his job. Becker spent the rest of his life working on his books and educating the public, and died in 2008. His books should be on every electrosensitive's reading list. They take some brainpower to get through, but can give you a better understanding of how the body operates electrically.

Fast-forward to the modern era and there's this new guy, Michael Levin, who's doing experiments that are eerily similar to Becker's work...yet he is celebrated by the medical establishment. Levin, who has bachelor's degrees in biology and computer science from Tufts University, and a Ph. D from Harvard in genetics, is a synthetic biologist working at Tufts University. He looks and speaks like a "tech-bro," and is making bioelectricity almost a buzzword.

In his lab, Levin has experimented with limb regrowth in salamanders and frogs, and is now experimenting with limb regrowth in mice. Like Becker, Levin also worked with Planaria, cutting them into pieces and watching them regenerate new heads or tails, depending on how he's manipulated their electrical circuitry, which he does by turning on and off the ion channels with drugs instead of by applying voltage. An interesting aspect of Planaria is that they use somatic inheritance, which means that mutations that happen during the flatworm's lifespan and thus are not on the DNA, such as acquiring two heads, is passed on to the next generation. That would be like if you got a tattoo, and then your children were born with the same tattoo. Where is this information stored, if not on the DNA? Levin says that it is "kept as electrical memory in the electrical circuit and sub-cellular architecture of cells."

The DNA, according to Levin, is the recipe for the cell's hardware (the proteins, enzymes, etc.) but it doesn't code for the shape and overall design of the organism. This comes from electricity: "When you turn on the juice, it reliably turns on a pattern of activity." This activity is reprogrammable, which Levin proved in his lab by taking frog skin cells and letting them do their own thing. The cells, which he calls xenobots or biological robots, run mazes and self-assemble, showing intelligence and behaving like a completely different organism. They self-assemble on their own into clumps of cells, or, Levin and the other scientists in the lab can make a computer model of an organism or a tissue they want to build, and then tell the xenobots to assemble into this thing.

The xenobot research is still in its beginning stages, but Levin envisions an "anatomical compiler," like a 3-D printer for biological tissues: map out whatever you want to create, and the computer would assemble it out of cells. That sounds great if I want a new liver or new teeth. But what happens when the lab director's eight-year old boy with artistic talent and a great imagination sneaks into the office?

At their most basic level, biology and computer science are the same field, Levin says. He uses terms like competency, pursuit of goals, and computational capacity, to describe biological systems. I don't think he's wrong. It really is just a bunch of 1's and 0's, electrical switches that are either off or on. He's interesting to listen to, and I recommend it: he says things that make me think. Although my philosophy of life is quite different and I think the xenobots are creepy, I can't argue with Levin's logic that life is a "bioelectric code" that we one day could crack. And I think it's interesting that he talks about "unconventional cognition," and ascribes "cognition" (not to be confused with "consciousness") to plants as well as to robots.

"If your neighbor got a brain implant that allowed him to mentally run a vacuum cleaner- no big deal- and your other neighbor had a vacuum cleaner that had some human brain cells that enabled it to get around- also no big deal, still pretty much a vacuum cleaner- so in most cases, a 90/10 split is no big deal. But what about a 50/50 split? So I think this idea of what a machine is, what a human is, these definitions are not as robust as we think they are." Wow, and I thought I had it bad with Roomba.

So, why is Robert O. Becker's work forgotten except by electrosensitives, and Michael Levin is featured on NPR,

Wired Magazine, the New York Times, TED talks, and various mainstream biotech podcasts? Is it simply that times are changing, and people are willing to listen to an idea whose time has come? I checked out their Wikipedia pages to get some clues.

At first glance Becker's page seemed a matter-of-fact summary of his research and career accomplishments, and credits him as being the "father of electromedicine" who studied "electrochemically induced cellular regeneration." It talked about his early life, research, the books, and his awards. But then I looked closer: a message above the overview of his research warned that "this section may present fringe theories, without giving appropriate weight to the mainstream view." Uh oh, can't have that. The discussion of electrical potentials in the frog and salamander limb regeneration experiments seemed fairly straightforward...I read on. Oh...he mentioned external influences like earth magnetism and solar winds as his explanation for what turns on "the juice." And- gasp!- he said that acupuncture was real (after taking detailed measurements on the acupuncture points with a voltmeter). And then, the final nail in the coffin: "He has been named as one of the most influential figures in the area of anti-EMF activism."

Michael Levin's page has no such disclaimer. There's a picture of a xenobot and a mention that the xenobot work was funded by DARPA (the nice folks who also gave us the computer mouse, GPS, Siri, drones, The Internet, and 5G). It talks about using bioelectricity for cellular control, and using AI to create models of morphogenesis.

So I guess the conclusion is we can reduce life to an equation and can modify it to fit our digital world. AI can help us do that, and we can merge AI and biology. What could possibly go wrong? But, as soon as someone tries to modify our digital world to fit in better with our biological one, by opposing cell towers on kids' schools, for example, then you're a quack and you better shut the fuck up or you'll get cancelled.

Desert Rat makes a Nest

Okay, I'll try to explain how things are out here in this desert on the brink of nowhere. This is what daily reality is if you want (or need) a life without wireless technology. As I write this in 2022 (the ten year mark of my onset of electrosensitivity), the machine empire's greasy tentacles have infiltrated nearly every part of the globe. Very few places are safe for electrosensitives like me anymore. This desert is one of them. So far.

This valley feels like a land that time forgot. Or where time never existed. And I feel like I'm living in a (mostly good or neutral) dream that's lasted years.

Heat so intense the cats and chickens pant and all you can do is crawl under a juniper tree with a book and a flyswatter. Winters so cold you need two sleeping bags and a bunch of blankets piled up on top to get through the night. And then there's the other season, in between Heat and Cold: Wind. Also known as Fucking Wind. Like sixty mile an hour dust storms every day and sometimes half the night wind. It shakes the camper (if you're lucky enough to have a camper, that is, and not just a rock- I've had both), it blows away anything that's not tied down (watch out for sheets of metal roofing flying at you), and it leaves a layer of red dirt at the bottom of your coffee cup and the goats' water buckets. But at least it blows the gnats away.

My solar-powered well changes everything. I remember back in The Land days when my morning routine used to be walking to the stream every day to fetch water, bathe, and do laundry, and on the way back filling a bag with wild tumbleweeds and mustard greens to cook over a campfire (I miss those timeless days! Now, as a landowner with responsibilities, my days are a hectic scramble of filling water buckets for goats, feeding goats hay, trying to get goats to shut the fuck up, chasing goats out of my camper, chasing chickens, building fences to keep goats from wandering away, building houses for goats, etc.).

I don't have lights at night. I use a headlamp, in previous years I just went to bed when the sun went down. I don't have insomnia either. There is also no cell phone pestering me, no beeping appliances, definitely no Alexa (and if there was, I'd shoot it). No stench of Febreze or Glade plug-ins or any of the other awful things people keep in their homes. Just the smells of sage and juniper, maybe some goat shit.

There's red rocks and blue sky and howling wind and red dirt. There's phoebes nesting under the rafters in the spring. A species of fragrant lupine that lives only here. Coyotes howling in the hills at night. A billion stars. Cows mooing up a storm across the field. Rusted metal junk that cowboys left. Dead trucks as yard ornaments. Tumbleweed tornadoes. Tumbleweeds for dinner. More red dirt.

"What do you do for fun out here?" "Mostly just work." Or, watch clouds, or make rock art carvings, or read books, or drink strong coffee and shoot the shit for awhile with other hermits, or go for hikes in the ghost town and search for buried treasure, or go for barefoot runs in the snow, or yell at airplanes, or shoot guns, or learn the ID's of all those confusing yellow plants in the Asteraceae family, or pet the baby goats. But these days, mostly just work.

But it's work I want to do, driven by love. Exiled from civilization, so disabled by the wireless fields that, before I quit civilization, trying to do any job, anywhere, would put me at the risk of having a seizure, I now have a purpose in life out here on the edge of nowhere.

As I write this now at the end of 2022, the world as we know it is collapsing and a new one is forming, one that might be really bad...or, might be wonderful, if we can convince people to stop using toxic technology and come up with something better. I see lots of young people buying property and growing gardens, and I do think people want in their hearts to have a natural lifestyle. They just don't know how. I think the key is to turn off the digital alter (or hit it with a rock), and to ask yourself, what kind of world do you want for yourself and your children? Not what does social media tell you you want, but what do you want?

The digital dystopia that Elon and other agents of the Machine Empire promote will only come into existence if we consent to it. It is *not* inevitable. We do not need to be putting implants in our brains, or living in the Metaverse. As I set cedar fenceposts in the ground, I come across the old cedar posts from the people who lived here before me. I also find flint shards and stone tools from the culture that came before them. The present moment is a culmination of the decisions of everyday people. *We* create reality. I want a reality with goats and kitties and good music, with friends and gardens and wilderness, with safe communication options and fiber-optic Internet. I want a world where Yankee candles are only a distant memory, whispered in scary stories to children around the campfire. I can't control what other people do, but I can create a microcosm of this world for myself, and maybe it will catch on.

Or, then again, maybe it won't. Maybe I'll just be a hermit forever in this desert. That sounds okay too. Whatever. What keeps me going, what motivates me to get up in the morning and pound fenceposts and move rocks, is love, as I've said, love for all (biological) life. But, on those dark nights of the soul when I've got a pounding headache because someone got near me with their new 5G Smartphone and I'm wondering if there's any future left that is worth living, what keeps me going at those times is not love. It's just pure stubbornness.

Stubbornness, because I refuse to have a shitty life surrounded by people and their devices (and when your best friends are goats, you're going to pick up a few of their character traits). Stubbornness, because I refuse to let this shit kill me. I claim my right to have an awesome life, in nothing less than spectacular places. My fellow electrosensitives: If you give up and die or go on medication or just move back to town and get sick and crazy, that means the Dark Forces win and we lose. And I can't let that happen. Because *I* don't *ever* fucking lose.

Photo credit: Soula Marie

Are you Electrosensitive?

Are *you* electrosensitive? Do you feel anxious and just "not right" when you sit in certain spots in the house? Do you have other spots where you do feel okay? Are there places where you just can't concentrate? Do you get random fits of anger for no reason? What about random fits of anxiety? Do you have restless leg syndrome, or difficulty sitting still? Do you get a burning sensation if you use a cell phone or computer for too long? Do you feel nauseated by the stench of scented candles? Do you have muscle twitches or unexplained nerve pain? Do you throw up a lot? Do you get heart palpitations? Have you felt "not quite right" since the early 2000's? What about since 2020?

If any of these apply to you, you may want to buy or borrow an EMF meter and follow the advice given in the Meters chapter. Pay attention to how you feel in different electrical environments, and then use the meter to find the lowest EMF zone you can possibly find and camp there for at least a couple days (without your cell phone), sleeping on the ground if possible. How do you feel out there? Do you notice anything different when you go back to town?

If you think you are EMF sensitive, above all Don't Panic. Just pay attention. Stop supporting wireless technology with your dollars. You probably won't have to move under a rock. But get a landline. And keep your eyes open. Be aware of what's happening on this planet right now, in these "unprecedented times." And spread the word. We're all in this together.

(Photo credit: Soula Marie)

References

Reading List

The Invisible Rainbow: A History of Electricity and Life by Arthur Firstenberg.

Electronic Silent Spring: Facing the Dangers and Creating Safe Limits by Katie Singer

Cross Currents by Robert O. Becker

The Body Electric by Robert O. Becker

Wi-fi Refugee: Plight of the Modern Day Canary by Shannon Rowan

Healing is Voltage: Healing Eye Diseases by Jerry Tennant

Websites

www.bioinitiative.org A report on the relationship between EMF and health. https://electroplague.com. Personal stories of Wi-Fi refugees, and a list of sanctuaries.

https://magdahavas.com Research on biological effects of non-ionizing radiation. Be sure to check out the music videos.

www.onaraven'swing.com Website of En Terra photographer Ruth Davis

www.smartshelter.com Gary's website, hacked and removed by Telecom in 2008, but available on archive

Bibliography

"Bernstein Liebhard LLP Reports On Study That Finds More Cell Phone Radiation Side Effects." SF Gate, Home of the San Francisco Chronicle. June 12, 2012.

"Bobolinks navigate by Internal Compass." International Wildlife volume 14, number 6. 1984: page 28.

"Dr. Michael Levin: Biological Plasticity, Bioelectricity, and Limb Regeneration." Talking Biotech with Dr. Kevin Folta Podcast. Episode 342, April 22, 2022.

"Former Microsoft Canada President Challenges Telecom on 5G Safety." Environmental Health Trust. April 28, 2021.

Levin, Michael. "The Electrical Blueprints that Orchestrate Life." TED Talks Science and Medicine. March 31, 2021.

"Michael Levin on Growth, Form, Information and the Self." Sean Carrol's Mindscape Podcast. February 1, 2021.

"Michael Levin: Biology, Life, Aliens, Evolution, Embryogenesis, and Xenobots." Lex Fridman Podcast. October 1, 2022.

Wikipedia: The Free Encyclopedia. Wikimedia Foundation Inc. Updated. 27 December 2022, at 23:34 UTC. Encyclopedia on-line. Available from https://en.wikipedia.org/wiki/DARPA. Internet.

Wikipedia: The Free Encyclopedia. Wikimedia Foundation Inc. Updated 2 March 2023, at 17:08 UTC. Encyclopedia on-line. Available from https://en.wikipedia.org/wiki/Electromagnetic hypersensitivity. Internet.

Wikipedia: The Free Encyclopedia. Wikimedia Foundation Inc. 7 December 2022, 13:23 UTC. Encyclopedia on-line. Available from https://en.wikipedia.org/ wiki/Electromagnetic Spectrum. Internet.

Wikipedia: The Free Encyclopedia. Wikimedia Foundation Inc. 4 June 2011, at 11:46 UTC. Encyclopedia on-line. Available from https://en.wikipedia.org/wiki/ Electromagnetic hypersensitivity. Internet.

Wikipedia: The Free Encyclopedia. Wikimedia Foundation Inc. Updated. 7 October 2022, at 11:19 UTC. Encyclopedia on-line. Available from https://en.wikipedia.org/wiki/Robert O Becker. Internet.

Made in the USA
Las Vegas, NV
17 March 2025